14/04   £3.99

Gift Aid item

20 **12528415** 7101

CONSERVATIVE RADICALISM

CONSERVATIVE RADICALISM

*A Sociology of Conservative Party Youth Structures
and Libertarianism 1970–1992*

Timothy Evans

Berghahn Books
Providence • Oxford

First published in 1996 by
Berghahn Books

Editorial offices:
165 Taber Avenue, Providence, RI 02906, USA
Bush House, Merewood Avenue, Oxford, OX3 8EF, UK

Library of Congress Cataloging-in-Publication Data

```
Evans, Timothy, Dr.
    Conservative radicalism : a sociology of conservative party youth
structures and libertarianism, 1970-1992 / Timothy Evans.
    p.    cm.
    Includes bibliographical references.
    ISBN 1-57181-872-3
    1. Conservative Party (Great Britain)  2. Conservatism--Great
Britain.  3. Libertarianism--Great Britain.  4. Student movements-
-Great Britain.  5. Students--Great Britain--Political activity.
6. Youth--Great Britain--Political activity.    I. Title.
JN1129.C7E93   1996
324.24104--dc20                                         95-49651
                                                             CIP
```

British Library Cataloguing in Publication Data
A catalogue record for this book
is available from the British Library.

Printed in the United States on acid-free paper.

CONTENTS

ACKNOWLEDGEMENTS

It would be impossible to acknowledge the assistance and support of everyone who has been consulted in the researching and writing of this book. For not only have there been a large number of people involved, but many key sources prefer to remain anonymous.

Of all those who have lent their time and support with this project, Dr Chris Husbands of the London School of Economics, Chris R. Tame of the Libertarian Alliance and my good friend Antoine Clarke deserve special mention.

Other individuals who deserve special mention include: Mark Allatt, John Blundell, Josephine Bryan-Brown, Dr Eamonn Butler, Jim Evans, Sean Gabb, Berendina Galloway, Dr David Gladstone, Marc-Henri Glendening, Teresa Gorman MP, Judith Hatton, David Hoile, David Lucas, Professor David Marsland, Douglas Mason, Brian Micklethwait, Professor Kenneth Minogue, Dr Madsen Pirie, Don Riley, Guy Roberts, Iain Smedley, Paul Staines, Dr Angus Stewart, Martin Summers, Robert Thomas, Russell Whitaker, Hazel and Sheila Young, and my mother and father Dennis and Diana Evans.

None of the above are responsible for any of the errors that remain; nor should it be assumed that any of them share Libertarian or even 'radical Conservative' views.

ABSTRACT

A Sociology of Conservative Party Youth Structures and Libertarianism: 1970-1992 describes and analyses one of the most important phenomena in modern British politics; the rise within the British Conservative Party of the young Libertarian New Right.

Tracing the Party's youth politics back to its roots in the Young Imperial League, it argues that today's Conservative youth activists defy the psychological categories popularised by observers such as Adorno in the 1950s, for whom the logical tendency of any form of extreme conservatism was ultimately fascism. And it argues that over the last twenty years a new type of Conservative activist has emerged who completely re-defines the Conservative paradigm.

While the New Right has been associated with a reactionary agenda of social and economic change, this study argues that so far as its young members are concerned their core values rest upon a radical agenda which is explicitly internationalist, individualist, culturally relativist, and secularist. Under analysis, many members of such groups as the Conservative Collegiate Forum, the Young Conservatives and the National Association of Conservative Graduates, oppose Christianity, nationalism, sexism and militarism, and severely question the Monarchy, the family, the police and all other forms of established authority. Institutions and beliefs which their seniors and traditional Conservatives more readily accept.

Adhering to a world-view which has more to do with individualist – or 'property rights' – anarchism, than any form of collectivist ideology, such as fascism, the study examines the social background and political psychology of the young Libertarian right, and concludes that they represent the antithesis of traditional Burkean thought. For while Conservatives have historically adhered to the authority of religion, prescription, instinct and communitarianism, Libertarians place their faith in the authority of reality, reason, man, and capitalism. As a school whose epistemology is reason, ethics – self-interest, and politics – anarcho-capitalism, the study argues that they represent an important post-modernist paradigm-shift in both Conservative thought and activism.

LIST OF TABLES AND ILLUSTRATIONS

LIST OF ABBREVIATIONS

ASI	ADAM SMITH INSTITUTE
CCF	CONSERVATIVE COLLEGIATE FORUM
CCO	CONSERVATIVE CENTRAL OFFICE
CIA	CENTRAL INTELLIGENCE AGENCY
CND	CAMPAIGN FOR NUCLEAR DISARMAMENT
CS	CONSERVATIVE STUDENTS
FCS	FEDERATION OF CONSERVATIVE STUDENTS
FUCUA	FEDERATION OF UNIVERSITY CONSERVATIVE AND UNIONIST ASSOCIATIONS
GLYC	GREATER LONDON YOUNG CONSERVATIVES
IEA	INSTITUTE OF ECONOMIC AFFAIRS
ISOS	INTERNATIONAL SYMPOSIUM ON THE OPEN SOCIETY
LA	LIBERTARIAN ALLIANCE
LCS	LONDON CONSERVATIVE STUDENTS
NAC	NATIONAL ADVISORY COUNCIL
NACG	NATIONAL ASSOCIATION OF CONSERVATIVE GRADUATES
NAFF	NATIONAL ASSOCIATION FOR FREEDOM
NUS	NATIONAL UNION OF STUDENTS
OPCS	OFFICE OF POPULATION CENSUSES AND SURVEYS
SCCO	SCOTTISH CONSERVATIVE CENTRAL OFFICE
SDP	SOCIAL DEMOCRATIC PARTY
SFCS	SCOTTISH FEDERATION OF CONSERVATIVE STUDENTS
SYC	SCOTTISH YOUNG CONSERVATIVES
TRG	TORY REFORM GROUP
UCCA	UNIVERSITY CENTRAL COUNCIL ON ADMISSIONS
YCs	YOUNG CONSERVATIVES
YIL	YOUNG IMPERIAL LEAGUE
YTS	YOUTH TRAINING SCHEME

INTRODUCTION

....

The purpose of this study is to describe and analyse an important recent development in modern British politics: the rise within the Conservative Party of what has been called the Libertarian New Right. Various studies have already been published on this phenomenon – for example, those of Levitas, Gamble and others,[1] but most of these are seriously flawed, in so far as they misunderstand the nature of the movement that they purport to be examining.

For many, the words 'New Right' are associated with a reactionary – and, indeed, a nakedly oppressive – agenda of social and economic change. New Rightists are said to believe in a reassertion of traditional values. They are thought to be Christian, nationalist, sexist and militarist, supportive of the Monarchy, the family, the police and all other established institutions of authority. They dislike socialists, liberals, trade unionists, feminists, homosexuals, blacks and anyone else who enjoys, or supports the right to enjoy, an alternative way of life. And their agenda is thought to be implemented in two ways: first, by free-market policies, which will subject the most vulnerable members of society to the disciplining force of middle-class employers and managers; second, by strengthening the power of the State – to ensure obedience to the laws of the market, and directly to coerce those middle-class dissidents who cannot be reached by the market. What combination of these ways is used depends wholly on a pragmatic assessment of the circumstances, since the New Rightist cannot appeal beyond his prejudices to any coherent philosophy.

Following this kind of analysis, the New Right has often been popularly aligned with Fascism and South African apartheid. However, the truth is entirely different. The mainstream within the British New Right explicitly rejects such values. It is instead internationalist, individualist, culturally relativist, and secularist. Its adherents regard racism, sexism and nationalism as no more than different forms of the collectivist ideology to which they are implacably opposed. They argue that these ideas are 'holistic', because they subsume the individual in a wider collective whole. Far from wanting the State to persecute alternative lifestyles, they are active in the campaigns to legalise soft and hard drugs, pornography, and every consensual sexual act. Their advocacy of the free market has nothing to do with imposing discipline at second hand, and everything to do with reducing – and in some extreme instances, totally eliminating – the power of the State over the individual.[2]

Rather than fascism, this ideology most closely resembles nineteenth century classical Liberalism, from which it draws much of its inspiration, and on which it is often self-consciously an improvement. It can be found in its purest form in the Libertarian Alliance, a free-market think-tank led by an anarchist, Chris R. Tame, whose openly acknowledged interests range from the history of classical Liberalism to Elvis Presley and black rhythm and blues, and from various forms of martial arts – to exposing the Nazi roots of anti-smoking – and other health activist – campaigns.

How, though, could such a basic misunderstanding as this have occurred? One explanation is ignorance. From conversations with many lecturers across the United Kingdom who teach units on the New Right or anarchism or both, it became clear to the author that course reading lists are empty of such anarcho-capitalist thinkers as Josiah Warren, Ezra Heywood, William B. Greene, J. K. Ingalls, Stephen Pearl Andrews, Lysander Spooner, Benjamin Tucker, Max Stirner, David Friedman (son of Milton Friedman), and Murray Rothbard. Equally, the minimal state or 'Minarchist' school of classical Liberal thought is virtually ignored: though Robert Nozick is sometimes to be found on reading lists, important works such as those of the American novelist and philosopher Ayn Rand are hardly ever to be found.[3]

With ignorance, moreover, must go a conceptual failure common in most forms of modern political debate. Since 1789, following the seating arrangements in the French Estates General, the practice has spread of representing all political opinion on a spectrum ranging from left to right. On the right are supposed to be the Conservatives and reactionaries, on the left the Liberals and Radicals. The further away from the centre one is placed, the more extreme one's orientation. Since the New Right is, by definition, on the right, it is difficult to conceive how it can be anything but at the least a Conservative movement. Since it is placed on the extreme right, it is conceived depressingly often to be automatically Fascist in orientation.

This ignorance means that much analysis begins with the categories laid down in the 1960s and before by observers like Adorno, for whom the logical tendency of Conservatism is Fascism, and the Conservative himself mentally ill, his intellectual processes a symptom of certain unpleasant experiences in childhood.[4] Though such opinions have not been generally accepted, a consensus view of the conservative did emerge among sociological writers of an alienated or repressed individual, driven by his own inner insecurity to intervene in the lives of others.

Even those writers aware of a Libertarian stream within British conservatism tended to dismiss it as unimportant. Samuel Beer, for example, argued that State intervention and conservatism were logically connected, since:

British Tories are in some degree collectivists, not only in certain aims of policy, but also in certain methods of political action. Old traditions of strong government, paternalism, and the organic society have made easier the massive reassertion of state power that has taken place in recent decades, often under Conservative auspices.[5]

The resulting failure of understanding has been most marked in sociology, but can be found in a greater or lesser degree in such other subjects as economics, politics and philosophy. This failure has been disadvantageous to the New Right in at least two respects. In the first place, it has prevented any real criticism of its doctrines by the collectivist opposition. While a good general always attempts to know his enemy, it is clear that many Marxist, Conservative and ordinary 'middle-of-the-road' thinkers do not, as yet, fully understand what it is that they are opposing. This can lead to unusually easy victories when the two sides engage in debate. It can, indeed, induce a highly amusing state of shock, followed by intellectual paralysis, when some opponents learn in the course of debate what the New Rightists actually do believe. It can also, however, prevent the uncovering, and where possible the correcting, of flaws in the basic ideology – since, no matter what degree of self-criticism an ideology may encourage, its adherents must always be less competent at detecting such flaws than an informed opponent.

In the second place, academic misunderstanding can be a strong barrier against general understanding, since it is most usually at university nowadays that journalists and other workers in the media gain their theoretical frame of reference. Take, for instance, an interview with Teresa Gorman MP, conducted by Martyn Harris for the *Sunday Telegraph*:

She supported herself through teacher training college and university – 'My father was an iconoclast too: he wouldn't fill in the grant form' – and rose to become head of science at a London grammar school. She was politicised by a long visit to America in the 1960s – like coming from behind the Iron Curtain. There she first encountered the ideas of Hayek, Popper, Ayn Rand and other gurus of the New Right.[6]

What is important about this interview is how little the journalist knows of the ideology to which he is being exposed. For, attempting to understand this 'right winger', he writes: 'She is also, disconcertingly, a fan of the anarchist-socialist Ivan Illich ('just about my favourite author').'[7]

Similarly, in an interview with Douglas Mason, the influential domestic policy adviser of the Adam Smith Institute and 'father of the Poll Tax', the *Glasgow Herald* stated early in 1991:

Mason says that as a free marketeer he is for freeing us all from the shackles of Government and centralist control. 'I don't like being called a right-winger and seeing the Adam Smith Institute referred to as a right-wing think-tank. Freemarket is the word that should be used. Right-winger conjures up images like those buffoons in Cheltenham (where expatriate Scot Bill Galbraith had just been sacked from the Party for uncomplimentary comments on the local Conservative candidate who is black). I'm not interested in all that kind of thing. I don't have a position on race and immigration and so on.

'I suppose my logical end-position is anarchist' says Mason before leaving the lunch-table and braving the wet, cold and windy December elements dressed only in a smart pinstripe suit.[8]

While to the casual observer these might appear to be flippant examples, both Gorman and Mason are influential thinkers who as libertarians transcend the political spectrum as it is traditionally conceived. Gorman, like many other radical free-marketeers, is well-versed not only in classical Liberal and anarcho-capitalist thought but also in much nineteenth-century anarcho-socialist literature. Mason, equally, must be taken seriously at his word. For there is no doubt that as one of the first libertarians in the Conservative student movement, he was heavily influenced by many libertarian authors – in particular, by Robert Heinlein's portrayal of an anarcho-capitalist world in *The Moon is a Harsh Mistress.*[9]

In seeking to correct this misunderstanding, I have endeavoured to concentrate less on the ideas of the New Right than on the means by which they have been introduced into the Conservative Party. My own experience, reinforced by the results of my academic research, has led me to the conclusion that their introduction and growing popularity shows a paradigm shift within the Party. There is no rigid border. There are many elderly Libertarians in the Party. There are

many young collectivists. Many of the young Libertarians avoid the
extremes of anarcho-capitalism, and show great diversity in attitudes
and points of view. Even so, there is a division between old and
young within the Party. The old are to a large extent, religious, patriotic, conservative (note the lower-case 'c'). The young tend to be secular, internationalist, radical. To this extent, the rise of the New Right
can be described as a matter of generational change.

The process has been continuing for at least twenty years. It has
been accompanied – and to some degree has been caused by – the
progressive failure of the social-democratic consensus that has
guided social and economic policies in the West since the end of the
Second World War. It has also been at all times fiercely resisted, both
from Conservative Central Office and by the collectivists within the
Party youth organisations. Though every new academic year has
seen its new – and often increasing – harvest of young libertarians
ready and willing to join the youth organisations, the Party establishment has struggled to benefit from the campaigning enthusiasm
of these young people without giving up its intellectual hegemony.

Such progress as has been achieved so far has come about
through a persistent guerrilla campaign. Local branches have been
infiltrated and captured. From this base, assaults have been planned
and made on the central institutions. The war between opposing factions has been savage and often spectacular, with reports of the
larger battles spilling into the media – though seldom reported from
any distinctively New Right perspective.

In this respect, the rise of the New Right almost exactly parallels
the slightly earlier rise of the New Left within the Labour Party.
There is the same perceived bankruptcy of the established ideology,
the same broad division between old and young. The parallels have
been enhanced by a conscious adoption by the New Right strategists
of the same 'entryism' made famous by the Trotskyite militants of
the 1970s. This has ensured that Central Office has proved inca-
pable of doing more than temporarily mute the voice of the Conservative New Right. Every shutting-down or remodelling of an
infiltrated organisation has been followed, after a short regrouping,
by a fresh infiltration.

I regard myself as almost uniquely well placed to describe this
process. I have been a member of the Young Conservatives and
Conservative Students, and remain a sympathetic observer of the
Party and its aims and objectives. These qualifications have ensured
that I was trusted by the population studied here and have been able
to obtain honest opinions in interviews and questionnaires, and to

gain access to many publications and meetings that would not have been readily available to outside researchers.

In any study of a movement so controversial as the New Right, bias is inevitable. Even so, a bias confessed – as is here the case – is a bias discountable. I may be part of the Party that I am examining. I will say, however, that I am not therefore unaware or uncritical of the sometimes problematic nature of the free market; and am happy to discuss objections as and when they occur.

I will also stress the lack of any strictly teleological framework in my thesis. I am not convinced that the New Right will inevitably one day dominate the Conservative Party. History is too unpredictable, events too open to sudden and unexpected changes of course, for any such confident assertion to be made. Just as the New Left was thrown back in the 1980s, so the New Right may be kept out in the 1990s and beyond.

Avoiding predictions of future hegemony, I conclude, I hope more modestly, that the domination of the Conservative youth groups by various extreme libertarians shows most of the literature dealing with the political psychology of Conservative activism to be inadequate and out of date. The identification with authoritarian and paternalist collectivism does not explain the actions and beliefs of many members of the modern Party.

I hope that my study will be received as a well-informed and empirically accurate analysis and that it will be useful to sympathisers and enemies alike in studying the real sociological and political psychology of the New Right.

Notes and References

1. Levitas, R., (1986) 'Tory Students and the New Right', *Youth and Policy*, No.16. Gamble, A., (1979) 'The Free Economy and the strong state: the rise of the social market economy', in Milliband, R. and Saville, J., (eds) *The Socialist Register*, London, Merlin Press. Bosanquet, N., (1983) *After the New Right*, London, Heinemann. Levitas, R., (ed.) (1986) *The Ideology of the New Right*, Oxford, Polity Press.

    Concentrating on the work of Andrew Gamble, to illustrate the frequent academic mis-categorisation of the New Right, Alexander Shand noted: 'Andrew Gamble writing in 1979 on the newly elected Conservative government chose to describe the doctrine put forward by the Institute of Economic Affairs, Milton Friedman, and economic commentators such as Samuel Brittan, and rather surprisingly Hayek, as the 'social market economy'.' See: Shand, A. H., (1990) *Free Market Morality: The Political Economy of the Austrian School*, London, Routledge, p. 173.
2. Perhaps the most important point that could be made here is that many, and possibly most of those who have been labelled by the term 'New Right' do not see themselves as 'right-wing'. This applies even to some of those who have had books

published with 'New Right' in their titles. A number of authors complained that such titles were forced on them by publishers who felt the term was 'fashionable' or marketable, and they were often faced with the dilemma of either getting published under a title they disliked or not getting published at all. Such so-called New Right-ists saw themselves not as 'right-wing' but as liberals or libertarians or anarchists, and resented deeply being hurled into a category that included traditionalist con-servatives, authoritarians, racists, national socialists and fascists! This is precisely the argument of Chris Tame in his 'The New Enlightenment', in A. Seldon (ed.), (1985) *The 'New Right' Enlightenment*, Sevenoaks, Kent, Economic and Literary Books, and his 'Freedom, Responsibility and Justice: The Criminology of the 'New Right', in Stenson, K. and Cowell, D. (eds), (1991) *The Politics of Crime Control*, London, Sage Publications. The attribution of the term 'New Right' to Tame's essay was another example, in this case disputed by the author in the text itself, of this phenomenon.

3. Indeed, it can be argued – convincingly in my view – that the concept of the 'New Right' was largely socially constucted by socialists and Marxists. It was certainly a useful weapon against liberals and libertarians to try and lump them together with extreme authoritarians. Sometimes this was clearly a result of ignorance or simple ideological blindness, but at other times of delilberate malilce. An example of the latter can be seen in Gordon, P. and Klug, F., (1986) *New Right, New Racism*, London, Searchlight Publications. The title of this book accurately sums up the type of impression it wished to create. It was produced by tthe so-called 'anti-fascist' maga-zine *Searchlight*, which has become notorious for its inaccuracies, outright fabrica-tions and involvement in disreputable activities and attempts to smear libertarians, anarchists, social democrats, or Conservatives as 'anti-semites', racists, fascists, or Nazi fellow travellers. It is surprising that some scholars and journalists still seem to consider this journal a reliable source. Increasing numbers of commentators on the left however, are becoming aware of its unreliability, hidden agendas and involve-ment in fabrications. See for example, O'Hara, L., (1994) *A Lie Too Far: Searchlight, Hepple and the Left*, London, Mina Enterprises; Cambell, D., et al., 'Destabilising The Decent People', *New Statesman*, 15 February 1980; *Black Flag*, Nos. 155, 156, 160, 1985–86; Ramsay, R., 'Our Searchlight Problem', *Lobster*, No. 24, December 1992.

4. Adorno, T. W., et al. (1969) *The Authoritarian Personality*, New York, Norton Library.
5. Beer, S., cited in Norton, P. and Aughey, A., (1981) *Conservatives and Conservatism*, London, Temple Smith, p. 84.
6. The *Sunday Telegraph*, 27 May 1990, p. XXII.
7. Ibid.
8. *Glasgow Herald*, 7 January 1991.
9. Heinlein, R., (1969) *The Moon is a Harsh Mistress*, London, Hodder and Stoughton Ltd, New English Library.

*This book is dedicated to my mother and father,
Dennis and Diana Evans, with all my love and thanks.*

Chapter I

THE CHANGING FACE OF THE CONSERVATIVE PARTY

The Rise of a 'New Wave'

....

1.1 The Distant Origins of Conservative Youth: Brief Introductory History

Conservative Party youth politics can be traced back to the turn of the century and the establishment of the Young Imperial League (YIL). While by no means as structured or as influential as its post-Second-World-War offspring, the Young Conservatives (YCs), the Young Imperial League nevertheless enabled many youngsters to taste formal Conservative Party politics for the first time. As its name suggests, it aimed to foster and encourage Conservative support for 'Empire, King and Country' and espoused what many of its members thought to be the cardinal values of duty, honour, and service to one's country. However, with no formal income or grant from the Party's central organisation, it depended to a large extent on local Conservative Association generosity. Unlike today's YCs, with their often hectic and headline grabbing meetings, the Young Imperialists held no national conferences, no spectacular or expensive rallies. At a time when young people were to be seen but not heard the Young Imperialists acted accordingly and caused their elders little concern.

Because of the YIL's early success, the party decided in 1931 to set up another youth group aimed at attracting university undergraduates: the Federation of University Conservative and Unionist Associations (FUCUA), which was structured to operate separately in

---

Notes for this section begin on page 13.

individual universities, with its branches affiliated directly to the National Union of the party. A forerunner to the more democratic Federation of Conservative Students (FCS – established 1967), FUCUA however was never designed to be a nationally integrated or democratic body; for example, its chairmen were always appointed directly by the party's vice-chairman responsible for youth.

Unlike today's young Conservatives, members of both the YIL and FUCUA had little real power or status. Their organisational structures meant they were tightly controlled from the party's centre at all times and consequently they had no real means of contributing actively to the wider world of adult politics or policy formulation.

Arguably it was not until the late 1940s that the party began to treat its younger members as serious assets. After the Second World War and the defeat of Churchill in the 1945 general election, R. A. Butler was charged with the task of restructuring and modernising the party. Recognising the manpower advantages to be gained from involving large numbers of young people, Butler swiftly replaced the anachronistic YIL with the 'more forward-looking' Young Conservatives, an organisation that during the late 1940s and 1950s grew to enormous dimensions, becoming the largest ever political youth movement a democratic country has ever seen.[1]

As the party gave more powers and higher levels of status to its youth groups so it became increasingly clear during the 1950s and 1960s that it saw them as important suppliers and training grounds of its future political élite. As we shall see later, Conservative youth leaders were actively encouraged to stress such values as the necessity for strong leadership, duty and communitarian service, ideas at the very heart of early-twentieth-century Conservative Party psychology.

1.2   The Political Psychology of Early Twentieth-Century Conservative Party Politics

Although many writers have found it difficult in the twentieth century to define Conservatism, substantial agreement exists that its core values emanate from Edmund Burke.[2] Under Burke's theory, man is regarded to be basically a religious animal, and religion the foundation of civil society. Society itself is viewed as the natural, organic product of slow historical growth. Existing institutions embody the wisdom of previous generations, and right is a function of time. 'Prescription', as Burke put it, 'is the most solid of all titles'.[3] Man is argued to be a creature of instinct and emotion as well as reason. Prudence, prejudice, experience and habit are better guides than reason, logic, abstraction and metaphysics. Truth exists not in universal propositions but in concrete experience. Except in an ultimate moral sense, men are unequal. Social organisation is complex and always includes a variety of classes, orders and groups, differentiation, hierarchy and leadership being the inevitable products of any civil society. For Burke, as for most Conservative Party members during the earlier part of the twentieth century, the politics of community were superior to the individual. The rights of men were derived from their duties, and evil was rooted in human nature, not in any particular social institution.

Given this philosophical background, Conservatism has traditionally stressed the inevitability of classes and leadership in society. Historically, many Conservative Party members, both young and old, have consistently used the politics of nationalism, paternalism and even imperialism to legitimate their views. The Party's electoral fortunes after 1880 were built upon the projection of the Party as an integral part of the Union, the Empire, and the Constitution; and on the identifying of it with the established institutions and symbols of national legitimacy. National issues and causes were used to great effect to rally substantial sections of working-class and trade-unionist support, as Andrew Gamble noted:

The Conservatives presented themselves as the party of the national economy and the state, the party of the community rather than the market, the party of protection, imperialism, paternalism, and interventionism, not the party of free trade, cosmopolitanism, self-help, and laissez-faire. Before 1914 Tory hostility to liberal political economy was pronounced, particularly because it promoted individualism and questioned the authority of established institutions, and encouraged selfishness and competition between individuals and classes. The Conservatives believed that there were some things worthy dying in the last ditch for – the Union of the United Kingdom and the rights of property being two – but the preservation of an egalitarian and competitive market order was not among them.[4]

Intellectually, Conservatives were renowned for their hostility to doctrine at this time, and for their lack of principle. Churchill once described the party as:

A party of great vested interests, banded together in a formidable confederation … corruption at home, aggression to cover it up abroad; the trickery of tariff juggles, the tyranny of a party machine, sentiment by the bucketful; patriotism by the imperial pint; the open hand at the public exchequer, the open door at the public house; dear food for the million, cheap labour for the millionaire.[5]

At the time when the Young Imperial League was being established the politics of Empire preoccupied Conservatives. In 1923 the

Tory MP Leo S. Amery argued that a distinctively Conservative view of economics had to rest upon the principles of nationalism and imperialism; he asserted:

... the historical, national and Imperial conception of economics is essentially part of the whole Unionist, Conservative, or, to use a good old time-honoured name, Tory political creed. That creed is based not on the abstract political or economic rights of individuals or of classes, but on England and Englishmen, living realities with their history, their institutions, their character, their possibilities, set in the wider framework of the British Empire. And as such it differs fundamentally from both the other political creeds far more than they differ from each other. For all their apparent outward difference Liberalism and Socialism are essentially akin in virtue of their abstract, theoretical, non-national character.[6]

The YIL was established at a time when such ideas were prevalent. The politics of nationalism, deference and duty were tied to the realities of empire, mass production and cultural segmentation. Given that Conservatism rested during this period upon such holistic notions as the subsumation of the individual to the politics of the community, nation and empire, it is perhaps understandable that in the 1930s many leading Conservatives accepted the fashionable case for greater social planning and state intervention. At a time when Keynes was arguing that politicians should run society through the principles of 'management by an intelligent élite', many Conservatives found it attractive to argue for a so-called 'ordered middle way' between orthodox socialism and laissez-faire liberalism. It was in this world of pre-Popperian thought that Harold Macmillan wrote:

The next step forward, therefore, in our social thinking is to move on from 'piece-meal planning' to national planning – from the consideration of each industry or service separately to a consideration of them all collectively.[7]

He went on:

Expert criticism has revealed the deficiencies of partial or piecemeal planning, and has made it clear that we must carry the idea of planning further, and evolve such a national scheme. We must take account of all the problems, and of all the repercussions of partial schemes with limited objectives. If we do not widen its scope, the whole idea of planning will be discredited.
    ... The weakness of partial planning seems to me to arise from the incomplete and limited application of the principles of planning. The lesson of these errors, which I regard as errors of limitation, is not that we should retreat. On the contrary, we must advance, more rapidly and still further, upon the road of conscious regulation.[8]

Another Conservative commentator, Reginald Northam, also argued in favour of more planning and economic intervention. In his 1939 book, *Conservatism The Only Way*, Northam argued:

... a prime consideration of the State must ever be to attempt to secure such conditions as will as produce the greatest employment, for it is in that way the national wealth can be most effectively produced and distributed.

... The emphasis must be on man, on human values and not on material values. Economic forces which would have an anti-social effect must be checked by the authority of the State. National wealth can be measured in terms of £ s. d. It can also be measured in terms of human happiness.[9]

Northam articulated a Conservative creed typical of his generation. State intervention, the individual's service to the community and an idealised view of traditional rural English life were all key ingredients:

Action by the State in determining the flow of trade which we have seen in these post-war years, is more typical of our traditional outlook than the laissez-faire attitude of previous generations.

... The responsibility of the individual is to realise his duty to the community into which he has been born, in order, not only that he may become the biggest he can become in that community, but also that the rights which our forefathers gained for us through service may be retained for us and may be passed on to those who come after us.

... An attempt should be made to get back the spirit, although, may be, not the form of the old culture of rural England. The music and dancing and pageantry and other typical activities are of far greater importance than the cinema can ever be.[10]

Until recently many have popularly regarded this view of the world to be the stuff of Conservative Party politics. For the sceptics, traditional Conservatism has been something of an intellectually shallow project, as Philip Norton and Arthur Aughey suggested in their book, *Conservatives and Conservatism*:

Paternalistic Toryism views political development in a democracy in terms of securing a stable and continuing relationship between governed and governing. It seeks to portray Conservative politics as the assurance of national interest and social justice based upon enlightened and beneficent leadership by a natural elite. At the heart is the necessity of hierarchy and distinction and a leadership that inspires confidence and trust in the hearts as well as the minds of the citizenry. Like Sir Alec Douglas-Home's famous remark about his matchsticks, paternalistic Toryism is not very much concerned with economics at all but with the moral and social wellbeing of the nation within a stable order of reciprocal rights and duties. Its prevailing codewords include loyalty, honour and integrity. These qualities are said to inhere not in meritocratic cleverness or intellectual brilliance but in a practical wisdom and a social ease which is the essence of good leadership. It is thus much more concerned with character than with mere technical expertise; in Sir Winston Churchill's phrase, the paternalist feels that the role of the expert is not to be on top but on tap. The paternalistic Tory's view of the electorate is a belief that given the correct leadership the natural disposition of the British voter is to be deferential, that people desire security and wise guidance rather than rash social experimentation. The paternal style in Tory politics, to use the

terminology of McKenzie and Silver, appeals to the voter who prefers leaders to be of 'elite social origin' and takes a 'benign view of the upper class'.[11]

Throughout the 1950s, during the heyday of consensual paternalism, many academics thought the Conservative Party was inextricably tied to the 'out-dated' politics of the nation, the State, and the
family. As a political force, Conservatism was frequently thought of
as being a throwback to 'feudalism', and hence from the early 1950s
onwards a number of academics sought to analyse its supporters'
psychology in relation to such features as deference and authoritarianism. While most of this work was undertaken in the United States,
a great deal of it was relevant to Britain.

1.3   Adorno, Authoritarianism and the Problematic Nature of the Political Psychology of Conservatism

Reading Adorno's *The Authoritarian Personality* it is difficult to imagine the possibility of a Conservative activist ever being associated
with a belief system that might be described as 'radical' in any way.
For Adorno argued:

The prototypic 'conservative' ... is one who supports the status quo and
resists changes in existing politico-economic power arrangements, who supports conservative values and traditions, who believes that labour is properly subordinate to employer or management.[12]

Analysing Conservatives in the United States, Adorno's study concluded that essentially there existed two dispositional groups: the
'genuine conservatives' and the 'pseudo-conservatives'. The 'genuine conservative' referred to the individual with a broad pattern of
thought. He is genuine because, whatever the merits of his political
views, he is seriously concerned with fostering what is most vital in
the American democratic tradition. He believes, for example, in the
crucial importance of the profit motive and in the necessity of economic insecurity. But he also wants the best man to win irrespective
of his social background. While he is resistant to social change, he
can still be seriously critical of national and political 'in-groups' and,
what is more, he is relatively free of the rigidity and deep-rooted hostility characteristic of ethnocentrism. On the other hand:

The ethnocentric conservative is the pseudo-conservative, for he betrays in
his ethnocentrism a tendency antithetical to democratic values and tradition.
... his political views are based on the same underlying trends – submission
to authority, unconscious handling of hostility toward authority by means of
displacement and projection onto out-groups, and so on. ... It is indeed

paradoxical that the greatest psychological potential for anti-democratic change should come from those who claim to represent democratic tradition. For the pseudo-conservatives are the pseudo-democrats, and their needs dispose them to the use of force and oppression.[13]

Although this typology is far from value-neutral, *The Authoritarian Personality* is interesting because it suggested that some extreme Conservatives believe: 'in extending the economic functions of government, not for humanitarian reasons but as a means of limiting the power of labour and other groups'.[14] Analysing the psychology of anti-individualism within the American Conservative movement, economic interventionism was clearly identified as a component of authoritarianism. While in Britain Conservative commentators spoke in the 1940s and 1950s of the need for 'management by intelligent élite' and argued in favour of more State welfare, Adorno suggested that in America a new type of extreme Conservatism had emerged which enhanced statism. The conclusion was reached:

This is not merely a 'modern conservatism.' It is, rather a totally new direction; away from individualism and equality of opportunity, and toward a rigidly stratified society in which there is a minimum of economic mobility and in which the 'right' groups are in power, the out-groups subordinate. Perhaps the term 'reactionary' fits this ideology best. Ultimately it is fascism.[15]

Adorno argued that all forms of extreme Conservatism were logically Fascist in orientation. And he concluded that the authoritarian personality type was in some sense 'sick'. The projection and rigidity thought to be characteristic of authoritarians was presented as being psychopathological and symptomatic of a deep-seated malaise arising from disruptive experiences, particularly with the father, in early childhood. Adorno and his colleagues felt so confident of their findings that authoritarianism was referred to as a 'disease',[16] his basic hypothesis being that authoritarianism was dysfunctional.

However, while paranoia, projection and neuroticism might be argued to be clinical examples of such disease entities, in reality it is very difficult indeed to distinguish between different types of psychopathology. As Brian D. Crabbe has argued:

A subject who, in a personality inventory, reports personal feelings of distress, may be doing so, not because he cannot function among people generally but rather because the people among whom he finds himself are ones who, for some reason or other, have preferences for forms of conduct which are contrary to those which are customary for him. Being neurotic may be an effect of social disapproval, not a cause of it.

It is possible then that authoritarianism is not itself a disease or symptomatic of a disease but that the attitudes people have to authoritarianism may alone cause the observed variations in the correlation between authoritarianism and psychopathology indices. Where authoritarianism is disapproved of, authoritarians will tend to become neurotic (or, putting it the other way, only neurotics will remain authoritarian). Where authoritarianism is not disapproved of, there will be no observed relationship with psychopathology. Where authoritarianism is positively approved of, it will be the low authoritarians who show up as more poorly adjusted.[17]

For all its flaws, Adorno's work is, however, important because it has powerfully reinforced a popular notion of right-wing extremism. Given that an individual's political ideology is based to some extent on deep-lying personality traits, a great deal of work has followed that argues that characteristics such as 'authoritarian aggressiveness' and 'vindictiveness' are at the ideational heart of all 'extreme right-wing' movements. For instance, using Adorno's definition of pseudo-conservatism, Hofstadter defined the American extreme right, in 1955, as a:

... dissent ... [which] can most accurately be called pseudo-conservative ... because its exponents, although they believe themselves to be conservative and usually employ the rhetoric of conservatism, show signs of serious and restless dissatisfaction with American life, traditions and institutions.[18]

Although a number of academics swiftly criticised this type of work for being methodologically flawed, most notably Christie and Jahoda[19] and Shils,[20] its conclusions have passed, as John J. Ray argues, 'into popular mythology'.[21] Over a decade after *The Authoritarian Personality* was first published, Gilbert Abcarian and Sherman M. Stanage produced their paper 'Alienation and the Radical Right' arguing that right-wing extremists could be explained in terms of alienation: 'when certain forces block the individual's quest for authentic, or true, existence, when he feels unable to shake off ... an abyss, within himself, and between himself and other men'.[22]

For Abcarian and Stanage the general concept of alienation was developed by employing four variables. Extreme right-wing activism was said to be motivated by: 'meaninglessness', 'normlessness', 'powerlessness' and 'social isolation'. Right-wing activism was explained as essentially a reaction to a radically changing and impersonal modernity. Regarding the first of these variables, meaninglessness, they argued:

The experience of the right-wing extremist leaves him in great apprehension regarding the 'absolutes' of truth, values and meaning. For he sees, often unconsciously, that traditional conceptions of such absolutes have atrophied or disappeared in the life of Contemporary man.[23]

Similarly, on the topic of social isolation, they went on:

Loneliness and solitariness, the hallmarks of social isolation, result from loss of a personal centre of values and standards of certitude, and the feeling of functional insufficiency and ineffectiveness.

Impersonality, emptiness and distrust come to characterise one's life ... Social isolation creates an obsessive interest in distinguishing between 'friends' and 'enemies', until preoccupation with that distinction frequently becomes the central concern of interpersonal relations.

General alienation as previously described manifests itself as political alienation when any of four mechanisms were adopted by individuals.[24]

Right or wrong, many journalists, academics and intellectuals believe that to be a right-wing Conservative means that one is in some sense an alienated or 'repressed' individual, a moral absolutist who wants to intervene politically in other individuals' lives so as to direct and control. There is little suggestion in the literature available for the development of a group of right-wing extremists who advocate a radical political programme based on the anti-authoritarian principles of explicit individualism.

One of the few authors to stress the role of individualism within post-war right-wing politics was G. B. Rush.[25] However, like many other commentators writing in the early 1960s, he always saw it as being constrained by Conservatism's alliance with big business, and therefore he never saw the possibility for the development of an extreme and explicitly individualistic Libertarian right. Going so far as to discuss Conservatism's principle of 'limited individualism' he concluded:

Right-wing opposition is directed primarily against government, whose function it is to administer aid and welfare programs. This opposition to government is not universal, however, since the extreme right tolerates and even supports certain functions of the state (such as the 'police function' and the maintenance of the 'market-place economy'). Corporate business which, in the classical 'laissez-faire' sense, may be regarded as detrimental to the individualism of entrepreneurial business, is also spared extensive right-wing attack primarily because it is a potential source of economic support for extreme right groups ... The individualism advocated by the extreme right is limited, however, since the right to act in one's own best interests would not be extended to all individuals. Those who would subvert what the right wing extremist regards as 'the greatest good', (e.g., liberals and leftists), as well as the non-productive and shiftless members of the society (e.g., most minority group members), would not be afforded the privileges of individualism.[26]

Rush emphasises the inherent corporatism of post-war Conservatism. And in Britain there can be little doubt that it has been historically associated with an arguably authoritarian collectivism. As Samuel Beer asserted, Conservatism's traditional predisposition to nationalism and paternalism meant that many of its supporters found it easy, during the post-war period, to express a sympathy for collective institutions organised by the state. He argued that state interventionism and Conservatism were logical companions because:

British Tories are in some degree collectivists, not only in certain aims of policy, but also in certain methods of political action ... Old traditions of strong government, paternalism, and the organic society have made easier the massive reassertion of state power that has taken place in recent decades, often under Conservative auspices.[27]

1.4   Capitalism, the Need for a Re-evaluation of Conservative Party Youth Politics, and the Political Psychology of British Conservatism

Although Conservatives have traditionally been associated with the collectivist values of paternalism and nationalism, and the holistic politics of communitarian duty, it is arguable that in recent years a new type of right-wing activist has emerged in the Conservative Party that completely redefines the Conservative paradigm. In a world well away from the earlier part of the twentieth century and beyond, today's Conservative Party's youth activists ascribe to a radical belief system based upon extreme Libertarian values. Because they are heavily influenced by an essentially secular, internationalist and individualistic belief system, the nature of what it is to be a member of the Conservatives has to be re-examined and extensively reassessed.

Over the last twenty years, an increasing number of young Conservatives have come to advocate such policies as the legalisation of prostitution, surrogate motherhood and the selling of human organs; the privatisation of money, the Monarchy and the police. Whereas Conservatism has traditionally been suspicious of idealistic internationalism and careful to maintain and conserve a national identity, there is now ample evidence that large sections of the Party's youth favour the Libertarian agenda of the international free migration of capital, labour and property.

It was Hirsch who argued, back in the 1970s, that the consumption ethic of modern capitalism was undermining the social order and the harmonious stability that were the traditional imperatives of Conservatism. Modern trends in the Western economies reflected in an extreme form 'the conflict between traditional morality, with its stress on duty and social obligation, and individual maximisation of consumption as a good in itself'.[28]

For traditional Conservatives, what is being relentlessly lost in the modern world is a sense of the quality of life, concern for the environment and the social disciplines and responsibilities that make for community harmony. As Norton and Aughey have stated:

... if the fear of pessimistic Toryism seems to portray a future of mindless consumption and social conflict, it feels helpless to influence it. The pessimistic Tory is, like Lord Coleraine, 'a man caught up in another man's dream, and unable to break out of it'.[29]

Increasingly, traditional Conservatives appear to cast a jaundiced eye over all measurers of legislation that would seek to reform the human condition:

There is a fatalistic presentiment of some deluge to come. The present institutional dykes containing the flood are not expected to hold out for ever. Like Elie Kedourie they view with resigned alarm current developments in the nation and wonder what, 'under such conditions, Conservatives will come to understand by Conservatism' in years to come. The tragedy for pessimistic Tories is that they have no confidence about the answer to that particular question.[30]

According to Mishan, modern Conservatives have long appeared to be caught up on the free-market treadmill where one must press ever harder economically if one is 'to keep up in the race' or even survive.[31] Fred Hirsch in *The Social Limits to Growth* noted how it was becoming increasingly difficult, in a system based upon ever-increasing consumption and privatisation of interest, to reconcile social responsibility with the individualistic relationships of the market which Conservatives defended.[32]

While Whigs or liberal-Conservatives like Mrs Thatcher have, in recent years, opposed the Party's pessimistic paternalists, and supported many free market policies, few commentators have discussed the possibility of such a philosophy being taken to its logical, 'anarchic' conclusion. Instead, they have felt more secure in subtly describing the nature of free market thinkers in traditional terms. So, for example, Norton and Aughey have pointed out that modern:

Whiggery in effect gets down to materialistic basics and appears to brush off all the old moralistic *faux frais* of Toryism. Whiggery desires to anticipate change, to be in the van of economic and political reform and thus to mould events in a way that most efficiently preserves the equilibrium of the productive dynamism of capitalism. It is concerned to be intellectually respectable and to be engaged in a battle of ideas with its opponents. Thus Whiggery appeals to the calculating mind and so tends to elevate intelligence and intellectual rigour above mere deference to tradition. It puts greater faith in efficient business methods than it does in the comfortable chaos of just trying to muddle through. Its ambience is certainly not one of the leafy lanes of England ... [33]

What is important here is what is not being said. While Hirsch, Mishan, and Norton and Aughey have been subtly suggesting that Capitalism has and will continue to demand profound changes in the

Conservative creed, the radical and revolutionary nature of this shift has never been examined empirically with regard to the Party's members. At a time when social democracy is replacing orthodox state socialism in Central and Eastern Europe, and the British left are assessing the implications of a new, so-called, 'post-modern' world, it is arguably time to examine the Conservative Party's young, so-called 'New Wave' and to explore its free market values and radical political psychology further.

1.5 The Role and Importance of Conservative Party Youth

However, before going on, it is perhaps necessary to answer the question: why are the Party's youth activists so important in the first place? To which it is possible to reply that as major political parties the world over have come to access and rely upon external pressure groups, think-tanks and advisors with high levels of expertise, so no party like the Conservatives can do without a young, articulate, and highly-educated intake. Not only has the Party come increasingly to rely upon its younger members to act as parliamentary research assistants in the House of Commons, but many are relied upon to staff sympathetic policy groups such as the Adam Smith Institute and the Institute of Economic Affairs; where, it is said, many of 'tomorrow's ideas' come from.

Indeed, Dr Madsen Pirie, President of the influential Adam Smith Institute, has argued:

… You pack up for life while you are at university or college and the goods you take on board have to sustain you through the journey. Very few people make major intellectual changes during the course of their adult lives, so obviously what is done in the universities is very important for the future of any Party like the Conservatives.[34]

Discussing the influential nature of Conservative Students, Iain Smedley, a former Chairman of the Conservative Collegiate Forum (CCF – established 1987), has similarly commented:

The Conservative Student organisation, with around ten thousand members in one hundred college branches, is the YC's 'other half' in the Conservative youth movement. It is sixty years old this year, and has traditionally been at the forefront of Conservative Party thinking. Conservative Students advocated privatisation, student loans and the Community Charge long before they were mainstream ideas in the Party.

The YCs and students provide the Party with today's activists and tomorrow's leaders.[35]

If – as it seems – people do pack up at university ideas that sustain them through the intellectual journeys of their lives it naturally follows that what today's Conservative youth activists believe is of profound importance for the political future of not only the Conservative Party, but the United Kingdom as a whole. However, to understand fully the nature and importance of Libertarian youth activism it is necessary first to go back and examine its rise within the Federation of Conservative Students in the period from 1970 to 1986. For it is here that the story of the transformation of what it means to be a Conservative Party member took off. It is here that Libertarianism began to permeate the organisation nationally and where some of its members embarked upon the ideological road to anarcho-capitalism.

Notes and References

1. According to Norton and Aughey: 'The YCs reached a peak of 157,000 members in 1949.' See: Norton, P., and Aughey, A., (1981) *Conservatives and Conservatism*, London, Temple Smith, p. 213.
2. Burke, E., (1912) *Reflections on the Revolution in France*, London, Dent, first published 1790. Burke, E., (1962) *An Appeal from the New Whigs to the Old*, New York, Indianapolis, first published in 1791.
3. Burke cited in: Stankiewicz, W. J., (ed.) (1964) *Political Thought Since World War Two*, New York, Free Press, p. 358. The example of Burke underlines the difference between what is called Conservatism in the English-speaking countries and what is called Conservatism in Europe. European Conservatism is quite clearly and wholeheartedly an anti-individualist, anti-capitalist ideological phenomenon, a reaction to the Enlightenment and to liberal individualism as both an analytical and normative perspective. See: Nisbet, R. A., 'Conservatism and Sociology', *American Journal of Sociology*, Vol. LVIII, No. 2, September 1952 and 'De Bonald and the Concept of the Social Group', *Journal of the History of Ideas*, Vol. V, No. 3, June 1944. Its collectivism in turn can be seen as a formative influence upon both the origins of sociology and indeed upon socialism and Marxism. Although there are elements of such perspectives in Burke's traditionalism, there are equally clearly many elements of both political and economic liberalism. See: Dunn, William Clyde, 'Adam Smith and Edmund Burke: Complimentary Contemporaries', *Southern Economic Journal*, Vol. VII, No. 3, January 1941. See also Connor Cruise O'Brien's recent biography, *The Great Melody: A Thematic Biography and Commentated Anthology of Edmund Burke*, London, Sinclair Stevenson, Chicago, University of Chicago Press, which portrays Burke as essentially a Liberal. The attempt to make of Burke an icon of extreme traditionalism, authoritarianism or 'pragmatic', unprincipled realpolitik by certain contemporary Conservatives is profoundly mistaken. Libertarians themselves have, with some glee, pointed this out. Thus, see Marks, P., (1994) *The Principled Libertarianism of Edmund Burke (1729-1797)*, Libertarian Heritage No. 13, London, Libertarian Alliance, and Thomas, R., 'Edmund Burke, Liberty and Drugs', *Free Life: A Journal of Classical Liberal and Libertarian Thought*, No. 21, November 1994, p. 7. The true heir to Burke is not William Waldegrave, with his quasi-Hegelian, statist, anti-free market pragmatism, but the late Michael Oakeshott, with his tolerant, economically liberal support for an open society.

4. Gamble, A., (1983) 'Thatcherism and Conservative Politics' in Hall, Stuart and Jacques, Martin, (eds) *The Politics of Thatcherism*, London, Lawrence and Wishart, p. 119.

5. Ibid., p. 119.

6. Amery, L. S., (1923) *National and Imperial Economics*, London, The National Unionist Association, pp. 11-12. It is curious how the existence and importance of this alliance of statist Toryism and state Socialism has fallen out of any widespread consciousness. One of the few studies can be found in Semmel, B., (1960) *Imperialism and Social Reform: English Social-Imperial Thought, 1895-1914*, Cambridge MA, Harvard University Press. There is a growing literature on eugenics, 'right wing' (i.e. anti-liberal, anti-Capitalist) social darwinism and paternalism. See: Searle, G. R., (1971) *The Quest for National Efficiency*, Oxford, Oxford University Press and (1986) *Social Hygiene in Twentieth Century Britain*, London, Croom Helm; Soloway, R. A., (1990) *Demography and Degeneration: Eugenics and the Declining Birthrate in Twentieth Century Britain*, Chapel Hill, University of North Carolina Press. Some socialist scholars are also beginning to reconsider the origins and nature of the rise of the welfare state in the light of such evidence. See: Skocpol, T., (1992) *Protecting Soldiers and Mothers: The Political Origins of Social Policy in the United States*, Cambridge MA, Belknap Press/Harvard University Press; Jamieson, L. and Corr, H., (eds) (1990) *State, Private Life and Political Change*, London, Macmillan; Dwork, D., (1987) *War Is Good For Babies and Other Young Children*, London, Tavistock Publications. The origins of the Welfare State increasingly looks less like the pure juice of human kindness and altruism, a liberation of the masses, and increasingly more like authoritarian social engineering for the sake of national strength, war or racial hygiene.

7. Macmillan, H., (1938) *The Middle Way*, London, Macmillan & Co, p. 176.

8. Ibid., pp. 10-11.

9. Northam, R., (1939) *Conservatism The Only Way*, London, The Right Book Club, p. 105.

10. Ibid., pp. 111, 115, 180.

11. Norton, P., and Aughey, A., *Conservatives and Conservatism,* pp. 72-3.

12. Adorno, T. W., Frenkel-Brunswik, E., Levinson, D. J., and Sanford, R. N., (1950) *The Authoritarian Personality*, New York, Harper and Row, p. 177.

13. Ibid., p. 182.

14. Ibid.

15. Ibid.

16. See the concluding chapter in Adorno et al, ibid. See also: Crabbe, B. D., (1974) 'Are Authoritarians Sick?' in Ray, J. J., (ed.) (1974) *Conservatism As Heresy*, Brookvale NSW, Australia and New Zealand Book Co., p. 198.

17. Crabbe, B. D., ibid., p. 201.

18. Hofstadter, R., 'The Pseudo-Conservative Revolt', in Bell, D., (1955) *The New American Right*, New York, Criterion Books, pp. 34-5.

19. Christie, R., and Jahoda, M., (eds) (1954) *Studies in the Scope and Method of 'The Authoritarian Personality*, Glencoe, Ill., Free Press.

20. Shils, E. A., 'Authoritarianism 'Right and Left' ', in Christie, R., and Jahoda, M., ibid.

21. Ray, J. J., (ed.) (1974) *Conservatism as Heresy*, p. 199.

22. Abcarian, G., and Stanage, S. M., (1965) 'Alienation and the Radical Right', *The Journal of Politics*, Vol. 27, November, p. 784.

23. Ibid., p.789.

24. Ibid., pp. 787-8.

25. Rush, G. B., (1963) 'Toward A Definition of the Extreme Right', in the *Pacific Sociological Review*, Fall.

26. Ibid., p. 64.

27. Beer, S., cited in Norton, P., and Aughey, A., *Conservatives and Conservatism*, p. 84.

28. Norton, P., and Aughey, A., ibid., p. 72.

29. Ibid., p. 71.
30. Ibid., p. 72.
31. Ibid., p. 71.
32. Hirsch, F., (1977) *The Social Limits to Growth*, Cambridge MA, Harvard University Press.
33. Norton, P., and Aughey, A., *Conservatives and Conservatism*, p. 63.
34. Dr Madsen Pirie, President of the Adam Smith Institute in a recorded interview with the author, early 1988.
35. Smedley, I., (1990) 'One Hell of a Party,' in: Gray, P., (ed.) *Campaigner: The Magazine of the National Young Conservatives*, London, Youth Department, Conservative Central Office, p. 20.

Chapter II

CONSERVATIVE PARTY YOUTH, THE LIBERTARIAN PARADIGM AND THE ROAD TO ANARCHO-CAPITALISM

....

This chapter begins with an examination of the politics and history of the Young Conservatives, and goes on to analyse the Federation of Conservative Students (FCS). It deals primarily with the period 1970–86 and the emergence of the Federation's Libertarian faction. Analysis of the FCS has been divided inter-generationally between two activist waves: 1970–78 and 1980–86. The chapter considers how the FCS came to think the 'unthinkable', and begins to address the question of where they drew their ideas from. Why, for example, did members of the FCS start, during the late 1970s, to support the legalisation of drugs, the privatisation of the Monarchy, and 'anti-racist' policies associated with international free migration, policies far removed from the traditional philosophical boundaries of Conservatism?

2.1 The Young Conservatives

If we exclude the National Association of Conservative Graduates (NACG) for the time being, the Conservative Party had, before 1987, two major youth organisations, the Young Conservatives and the Federation of Conservative Students.

As we saw in Chapter I, the YCs took their modern form when R. A. Butler reorganised the party just after the Second World War. As

---

Notes for this section begin on page 46.

there were few other places in society for young people to meet informally and socialise, it was not long before the organisation became
known as being primarily a social club and a marriage bureau. To
rectify this situation, and 'politicise' its members, policy discussion
groups were formed in 1960.[1] These groups existed for many years
at branch, area, and national level, and initially attracted some 11,000
members – out of an estimated total YC population of 120,000.[2]

   While this revised structure enabled the Party to claim that
'Young Conservatives throughout the country are able to transmit
their views on problems concerning politics and young people
directly to the top',[3] in practice, as Abrams and Little have argued:

> ... the contribution of the young to the life of the Party [was] carefully guided
> so as to preserve the autonomy of the 'top'. Thus, the questions discussed by
> the Policy Groups [were] pre-selected by the Party... there [was] no provi-
> sion for dissent; unacceptably radical ideas [were] likely to be quietly filtered
> out as 'impractical'.[4]

   Up until the mid-1980s the main themes of YC activism were
built upon the principles of leadership, responsibility and service;
not policy formulation. The party continually held 'leadership'
schools and 'leadership' courses. In one year in the 1960s it is estimated that over 3,500 'potential leaders' were trained.[5] For Abrams
and Little, who researched the YC movement during the mid-1960s,
the party held a subtle but firm grip over its younger members:

> ... it is only senior Young Conservatives who are offered effective access to
> the inner councils of the Party. All the area and national officers of the move-
> ment are over 25 and according to the National Secretary they are people
> who 'want to be respected'. It is these old young people who provide the
> leadership and discipline for the movement as a whole. By the time they
> achieve responsibility many of them are thinking in terms of a political
> career. All have been well-coached in the values of leadership. Of all Young
> Conservatives they are the least likely to embarrass the Party.[6]

Describing the political ethos of YC membership, Abrams and Little
asserted:

> It is our impression that most members ... remain almost apolitical; theirs is
> a diffuse, patriotic politics not the politics of Party conflict and policy-mak-
> ing; their Conservatism is compact of a feeling for the nation, for the monar-
> chy and generally for individual enterprise which they associate with the
> established order. Membership serves to consolidate rather than to activate
> their loyalties.[7]

   Throughout the 1970s, little changed within the YC movement;
their numbers simply declined. Whereas back in the early 1960s
they had sent policy reports to the Cabinet, asking for improved

state industrial training, the simplification of school-leaving procedures, and the subsidisation of sport,[8] fifteen years later they were
still essentially pragmatic social democrats at heart.

Abrams and Little's research (which also dealt with the Young
Socialists and Young Liberals) is important because it concluded that
most political youth activists were involved as the result of family
socialisation. They argued:

> British politics have not provided any major activating experiences peculiar
> to this age group. Of those who are active the great majority are merely con-
> tinuing a family habit of engagement in public affairs. Often the critical politi-
> cizing experiences that brought the family into politics lie three generations
> away, in the Dock Strike, the Revolution of 1905, the Great War. Activism,
> like everything else in British politics today, is largely a matter of tradition.

> We would conclude then that there is little reason to treat the young in
> contemporary Britain as a new political generation. The perceptions and ori-
> entations of the age-group as a whole are organised in an old frame of ref-
> erence. Young activists, whatever their first hopes, are constrained to work
> old institutions and accept old possibilities. The pace of change is set by the
> political parties. At all levels the young are caught up in the patterns of the
> past. British youth has no collective political self-consciousness. There has
> been no breakthrough and there is little prospect of one.[9]

Unlike the YCs, the Young Socialists and the Young Liberals, it is
arguably the FCS who, during the early 1980s, made a 'breakthrough' and revolutionised British youth politics.

2.2   The Federation of Conservative Students

The Conservative student movement was founded (see Chapter I) in
1931 by John Buchan.[10] Until the FCS's closure in November 1986
it was the official student wing of the Party, and was organised separately from the Young Conservatives. Supported mainly by subsidy,
its national officers enjoyed an office in Conservative Central Office
(CCO), and its membership consisted of affiliated Conservative student associations in individual universities and colleges of higher
education throughout Britain.

It was in the mid-1970s, during the era of 'stagflation', that the
FCS began to break the mould of post-war youth politics. Attempting to explain why Conservative students found Libertarianism so
attractive, former FCS vice-chairman David Hoile has argued:

> ... young people on the right came onto campuses and came up against a
> very consistent and very doctrinaire socialist ideology to which, at that stage
> in time, Conservatives on campus had no real coherent answer. As a result
> of encountering this maximum state ideology, with its inherent socialism, the

young ... right ... on campuses came up with and developed a minimum state ideology as a specific counter. And with that were able to counter a whole multiplicity of leftist arguments about health cuts, education cuts, and so on and so forth ... I think that largely accounts in macro terms for the emergence of the minimal statist ideology within Conservative Students.[11]

Throughout the 1970s significant elements within the FCS became ever more critical of post-war government policy and began openly to criticise the spirit of consensual pragmatism. It was at this time that the FCS began to campaign for a range of policies that were designed to undermine the post-war settlement and challenge established orthodoxy. As Britain's economic performance declined and serious philosophical questions were raised within the higher echelons of the Party itself, so important differences of opinion began to emerge within the FCS. Ruth Levitas has stated, from this time onwards: '... differences between those who espoused a "moderate" conservatism characteristic of the post-war period, and those who espoused a "libertarian" or right-wing position, are easily discernible'.[12]

In April 1974 a motion to replace or supplement student grants by a loans system was proposed by Michael Forsyth (then an FCS delegate from St Andrews University and later the MP for Stirling). Although the motion was defeated by the FCS conference it stands as one of the first recorded instances of Libertarian activism.[13]

In 1975 Libertarians tabled a motion to the Welsh Conservative Party conference, regretting that there was little sign of the 'new Conservatism' on which Mrs Thatcher had been elected as Party leader.[14] However, it was not until April 1976 that they experienced their first major victory, the election of Forsyth as chairman. Under his leadership, he clearly intended to change the FCS: '... from being quite a docile organisation into a campaigning one'.[15] Under his authority the Federation's objectives were clearly set. There were three main aims. Firstly, the FCS would strive to create a more responsible and representative NUS. Secondly, Conservative students were to pursue a strongly pro-European strategy, forging alliances with other European centre right groups. And finally, they would vigorously promote a radical free-market agenda espousing the principles of Capitalism.

At the Federation's 1977 annual conference, Mrs Thatcher praised the FCS, which was now claiming at least 200 branches nationally and over 16,000 members. As it lost its social image and began to politicise so it became bigger. Whether this growth was a consequence of the organization's new-found radicalism, or for some other external political reason, is impossible to say. Nevertheless the figures were impressive. In 1974 there had been only one Tory Student president; by 1977 there were at least fifty.[16]

While the FCS was being showered with praise by the Party's leadership, however, the Libertarians were preparing to pass a range of resolutions which they hoped would strengthen their position. Their agenda included such issues as the legalisation of cannabis, abortion (though not free) on demand, and wider rights for homosexuals.[17] Not surprisingly, these policies angered many in the party and CCO. Responding to the subsequent furore in the press, Forsyth was quoted as saying: 'The Federation is simply coming to terms with the dichotomy in some sections of the Conservative Party that says you should be free to do what you want with your private property but not with your private parts'.[18]

Attempting to counter his line, Ronald Butt writing in *The Times* alleged that Forsyth '... (and a lot of his members) would accept the legalizing of heroin – believing in any case that "openness" could reduce the number of people taking heroin'.[19] Butt argued that Conservatism was about 'order', not just freedom.

Forsyth's period as chairman was followed by the moderate, David Wilks. Under his leadership the Federation continued to campaign against the NUS but with far less vigour. The campaign was now one of reform rather than transformation.[20] A national campaign to make student unions more democratic was launched on 1 February 1978.[21] It demanded that union officials, conference delegates and members of student representative councils be elected by a comprehensive secret ballot involving all students. Wilks argued:

At the last National Union of Students conference in December, only 30 of the 317 universities, polytechnics and colleges which sent delegates had elected them by secret ballot; a fifth (61) by the student representative council and a quarter (80) by the union executive.

The student councils and the union executive had in their turn usually been elected at student union general meetings, which were usually attended by only a handful of students.[22]

Despite the continuing politicisation of Conservative students, and the gradual permeation by Libertarian cadres within FCS's organic structure, the Federation remained under moderate control for several years. Nevertheless, the Libertarians persisted and in early 1978 demanded immediate disaffiliation from the NUS.[23] They argued that because student-union membership was a closed shop, it was contrary to the values of a society based upon the principles of individual freedom and voluntary action. For all their power the moderates were not able to prevent many FCS members, perhaps influenced by the growing anti-closed shop organisation the National Association For Freedom (NAFF),[24] encouraging individual unions to disaffiliate from NUS; including most Scottish universities.[25]

At the 1978 FCS annual conference, held in Loughborough, the Libertarians maintained a sizeable opposition to the national leadership. Their strength was such that they were able to ensure a commitment to the legalisation of cannabis, abortion on demand, homosexual rights, and the removal of restrictions on adult pornography. Adopted the previous year, the so-called 'freedom motion' was retained in the face of fierce opposition from many on the left of the Party. Under the heading 'Tory student vote for liberty' Diana Geddes wrote in *The Times*:

Mr Stephen Jarvis, proposer of last year's freedom motion and a member of the National Association for Freedom, won much support when he argued that Conservative students must decide between a libertarian society, with the individual free to decide for himself what his morals should be, and a paternalistic society, with moral standards laid down by the state.[26]

Interestingly, the article went on to note:

Mr Norman St John-Stevas, MP, Parliamentary Spokesman on Education addressing the conference after the debate, expressed dismay that the discussion had taken place against no philosophical background.

Too much of the debate on issues such as abortion and drugs had looked at only one side of the argument, that of the individuals's rights, he said. He emphasised the danger of a collapse into a society that was totally without values, that rejected all objective moral standards.[27]

Despite the Libertarian influence within FCS, the Federation's leadership reverted to being so moderate that Nicholas Winterton MP described the Federation as 'pseudo-socialist' and their remaining within NUS as 'appeasement'.[28]

In 1979, as Mrs Thatcher began her first term of office, another moderate, Stuart Bayliss, took over as FCS chairman. The lone Conservative voice on the National Union of Students' executive the previous year, Bayliss was unwilling to steer the Federation rightwards and out of the NUS. Instead, he concentrated on working within existing structures and on boosting the FCS's membership *The Times* duly noted that the Federation had done much:

... to improve their organisation ... They have nearly 100 of the 700 student delegates at ... [this year's NUS] conference: membership figures are expected to be up by about 15% on last year; and with some 20,000 members, they are the largest political group among students, the left being splintered into factions.[29]

2.3 The FCS's Second-Wave Paradigm Shift: The Road to Anarcho-Capitalism

The Federation had a brief flirtation with Libertarian activism in the 1970s, but the real breakthrough occurred in 1980 with the election of Peter Young as FCS Chairman.

It was during the early 1980s that the FCS expressed a political world-view that went a great way towards 'bracketing out' many of society's commonly held moral judgments. Conservative students rejected much that had been previously thought of as 'Conservative'. And from 1980 onwards they used in Libertarianism a paradigm that not only fitted in with many of the 'anti-interventionist' elements of Thatcherism, but also opposed much of the intellectual left's 'egalitarian moralising'. For on the one hand, it extended the economic logic of Thatcherism, while on the other, it enabled the FCS ideologically to reject the 'political hypocrisy' associated with the emotive and statist concepts of nationalism, racism, sexism and authoritarianism. Second-generation Libertarians who took control of the FCS had new, radical and, of course controversial ideas, which quickly earned them the reputation of being 'extremists'.

In early January 1980, some few weeks before his election victory, Peter Young was arrested at Warsaw airport for attending an 'unofficial conference in Poland'. After being stripped, searched and held in police custody for seven hours, he told the press that Polish dissident journals and photographs had been forcibly taken from his rucksack. Young, aged twenty-one, and already the senior vice-chairman of the FCS (as well as the publicity officer for the all-party East European Solidarity Youth Movement), had been to a conference organised by leading members of the Polish dissident community with which he was closely associated.[30]

This episode greatly enhanced Young's reputation for being an effective and committed political operator, just at a time when he needed it. Although his subsequent election to FCS Chairman was, as the *Times Higher Education Supplement* put it, a 'surprise',[31] he nevertheless beat his rival Miss Anna Soubry by 127 votes to 118. Furthermore, Young's allies won eight out of the eleven posts on the FCS's national committee. Both sides in the election battle agreed that it had been the most keenly fought for many years, and marked by 'dirty campaigns'.[32] It was not long before Young made his political position clear: 'I was elected on an anti-NUS platform. Also taking a tough line against the left and for stronger ties with and support for the Government's policies'[33]

Under Young's leadership the FCS began to espouse the radical principles of *laissez-faire* Capitalism in a way that the organisation had never done before. It immediately demanded the termination of state funds to a large number of groups, including, amongst others, the British Youth Council, the Arts Council, and Youth for Peace (described by the FCS as a 'Soviet propaganda outfit').[34] Although Young had inherited a standing policy against the introduction of loans, in early September he stated that both he and a majority on the national executive were in favour of a loans system. The *Times Higher Educational Supplement* quoted him as saying: 'I have been in favour of a partial loans system for some time. The issue is not grants versus loans but introducing loans in place of say discretionary awards or parental contributions. Loans would provide extra money to finance studies.'[35]

In October, the national committee of FCS voted for a drastic reduction of the mandatory student grant to £500 a year and the introduction of a student loan scheme to make up the difference.[36] The committee recommended that the loans should be funded by private banks and that they should be repaid in the form of a graduate income tax. The motion was passed by five votes to four.[37] Not surprisingly, this caused a rift within FCS, especially between Libertarian executive committee members and many ordinary members at branch level. *The Times* reported: '... dissenting members said no concern had been shown for students but only the desire to equate all facets of society to a free market philosophy'.[38]

In late October sixteen FCS members issued a statement attacking the national executive committee for not consulting the membership and for being 'out of touch'.[39] The statement, signed by eight regional chairmen, three national committee members, and two members of the National Union of Students' executive, read: 'It is a pity that it is seen to be necessary to indulge in such misguided and ill-informed displays of political virility.'[40]

The 1981 FCS national conference, held at Sheffield University, and attended by more than 500 delegates, passed a motion that called for all tacit and active support of the NUS to be withdrawn immediately. This meant that the FCS, celebrating its 50th anniversary, would not be represented at its conferences and that none of its members would be allowed to stand for election to the NUS's executive. The FCS now supported all disaffiliation campaigns. Confirming the Federation's move to the Libertarian right, this conference elected hardliner Tim Linacre to follow Peter Young.

Linacre, who took over in the summer of 1981, beat his 'wet' rival, Peter Batey of Oxford University, by 265 votes to 233.[41] Noting the significance of the result Paul Flater of the *Times Higher Education Supplement* wrote:

The hardliners hold a comfortable majority on the new National Committee and with a clear mandate appear keen to launch a new offensive on the NUS. Scotland, where five out of eight universities have left NUS, could be the testing ground for an embryonic FCS-run national union.[42]

During Young's year of office British politics had clearly begun to polarise. As the economic recession began to bite, the government instituted severe public expenditure controls, unemployment rose dramatically and the left subsequently re-emerged on campuses in a way not seen since the late 1960s. At a time when Conservative economic policy was increasingly dominated by the principles of classical liberalism, the Labour Party, under the leadership of Michael Foot, moved to the left.

It was not long before a new Social Democratic Party (SDP) emerged. Led by Dr David Owen, the SDP soon attracted a number of 'Tory wets' including some who left the FCS. Tim Linacre's year of office thus began in the wake of a number of prominent defections, including three former FCS chairmen. The list included: Stuart Bayliss, FCS Chairman 1979–80; Eddie Longworth, FCS Chairman 1978–79; David Wilks, FCS Chairman 1977–78; Anna Soubry, Conservative member of the NUS executive from 1979–80; Tom Hayhoe, a former president of the Cambridge University Students' Union and speech writer to Peter Walker; Roy Evans, former President of Birmingham University Students' Union; Adair Turner, former Chairman of the Cambridge University Conservative Association and President of the Cambridge Union; and finally Mr Peter Blythe, a former Chairman of the National Association of Conservative Graduates.[43] According to press reports Bayliss and Hayhoe were so concerned about the general tenor of government policy and the ideology influencing the Prime Minister that they joined the newly formed Tory Reform Group (TRG) and were appointed to its national executive. Although the TRG had gained the support of Edward Heath it apparently failed to convince many Conservative 'wets' in the House of Commons of a need for a change of approach.[44]

There can be little doubt that these defections delighted many of the Thatcherite revolution's most ardent supporters, particularly in the FCS's Libertarian faction. Commenting on the situation at the time, Michael Forsyth wrote in a letter to *The Times*:

Sir, I was amused as a former chairman of the Federation of Conservative Students (1976) to read Ian Bradley's 'Young Tories defect to join SDP' (August 12). The individuals concerned included the three FCS chairmen

who succeeded me and whose period in office was characterised by a determination to turn the organisation into a student political party pursuing policies wholly at odds with those of the Conservative Party.

They consistently supported the communist-dominated 'broad left' line
on most issues at NUS conferences and their election successes depended
on communist help.

Mr Wilkes and Mr Longworth were responsible for introducing FCS to
membership of the Anti-Nazi League, a decision which was subsequently
overturned by their outraged membership. As for Mr Bayliss, he stood for the
union presidency at Nottingham University in 1976 as a Scandinavian Social
Democrat and refused to be aligned with the Conservatives in any way.

These individuals have never been committed supporters of Conservative policies and their so-called defection to the SDP is nothing more than
student politicians furthering their political careers. In doing so they are
emulating at least one of their contemporaries, Miss Sue Slipman, former
communist president of NUS.[45]

This letter is of interest not simply because it is indicative of the
emerging factionalism within the FCS, but it is important because it
is a rare – public – example of the growing Libertarian tactic to align
the 'wets' with 'communists'. Following the work of Hayek, many
within the FCS's Libertarian faction argued that the wets, and in
particular members of the TRG, were the natural allies of Communists (and Fascists) because they supported a political order that
inherently relied upon a large bureaucratic state. The Libertarian
world-view was such that during the early 1980s in some 'sound'
Conservative student circles the term 'wet' became obsolete, being
replaced by the interchangeable terms 'communist' or 'scum'.[46]

The press at this time attempting to describe the differences of
opinion within the FCS perceptively talked of the 'wets' and the
'arids'.[47] While rumours and statements continued to circulate about
how many other young Tory students would follow the initial batch
of defectors into the SDP, leading members of the Neasden Group,
representing moderate opinion inside the Federation, made it clear
that they intended to stay and 'fight their corner'.[48] The 'arid' FCS
chairman Tim Linacre welcomed the decision by announcing 'I
don't obviously agree with their political stance, but it is excellent
news.'[49] He went on: 'We intend to ensure that there are plenty of
avenues for them to make their views known. All the evidence however suggests that the vast majority of Conservative Students are
behind Mrs Thatcher's policies.'[50]

Paul Goodman, a spokesman for the Neasden Group and one of
two Conservatives on the NUS executive, said that the moderates
had no intention of defecting to the SDP: 'We want to fight to change
the FCS line', he said.[51] In August, the Neasden Group launched a

new lobby, 'Conservatives in NUS'. It aimed to ensure that Conservative students retained a voice inside the union, even though the Federation was now committed to its break-up. In a statement to the press Goodman argued: 'There has always been a Conservative voice in NUS because a majority of Conservatives think this is right. While everyone wants a reformed NUS, we do not support alternatives which will mean no NUS at all.'[52]

At the FCS half-yearly conference, the existing union membership system was condemned by Tim Linacre as 'abhorrent'.[53] FCS officers agreed to undertake research into a workable voluntary system with which they could lobby ministers. By late September a twelve page report, *The Truth About NUS*, was published. It argued that the NUS was 'undemocratic, unrepresentative and a waste of £1 million of taxpayers' money' a year.[54] Although a number of Conservative backbench MPs welcomed it, the government subsequently took no action.

Away from the NUS issue, much of Tim Linacre's year as chairman was taken up with a growing number of allegations about fraud within the FCS. Although the organisation had been the subject of a relatively small internal party inquiry, headed by Lord Thorneycroft, the year before (regarding allegations of vote-rigging),[55] a range of new allegations emerged that soon entered the public domain. In early April 1982 the National Union of Students wrote to the party Chairman, Cecil Parkinson, urging him to carry out an internal inquiry into the alleged forging of supporting signatures on the nomination forms of Conservatives standing in the NUS's annual election on an anti-NUS platform. According to Wendy Berliner of The *Guardian*: 'After inquiries among delegates who had supposedly signed the forms it became clear that 10 of every 15 signatures were fake.'[56] Soon after, the chairman of the FCS's Student Affairs Committee, resigned.[57] From the reports available it is clear that many hoped his resignation would leave the FCS to concentrate more on their political activities. However, by the middle of April new allegations emerged regarding serious financial malpractice and a host of other 'dirty tricks'. The newly elected 1982–83 chairman, Brian Monteith, therefore started his year of office under the threat of a fresh party inquiry. Alongside Monteith, himself a Libertarian, sat both Peter Young and Tim Linacre on the national committee.

It was not long before dissatisfaction with the FCS's leadership once again became apparent. The 2,500 strong Oxford and Cambridge Conservative Associations issued a resignation threat.[58] Under mounting pressure an inquiry was finally set up by CCO and headed by Anthony Garner, the director of the Party's organisation and community affairs department.

The Oxford and Cambridge Conservative Associations alleged that a bank account had been opened in the alias of Mycroft Holmes, the civil-servant brother of Sherlock Holmes, and that a slush fund had been used to finance bogus delegates to the 1981 conference in order to swell the right-wing vote.[59]

In July 1982 the inquiry concluded that Peter Young had opened, and was the sole signatory of, a secret bank account in the name of Mycroft Holmes, and that during a period of eighteen months more than £4,000 had passed through it. Furthermore, it was discovered that the money had been raised from business people between December 1979 and June 1981,[60] and that some of the money had been used to finance bogus delegates to the 1981 conference. Individuals had been bussed – free of charge – from far and wide to attend the conference and paid to 'vote the line'. The inquiry discovered that the money had also been used to finance the NUS disaffiliation campaign, which at Heriot-Watt University had cost more than £1,000.[61] Although the inquiry recommended constitutional changes, which would have resulted in a majority of the Federation's committee being elected regionally rather than by annual conference, these proposals came to nothing. Drawn up by Donald Walters, chairman of the Conservative National Union, it was not long before they were rejected by the FCS conference in September 1982.

Regarding the allegations of electoral malpractice, Brian Monteith was found guilty of 'grave errors of judgment',[62] but did not resign. The inquiry report concluded that as Monteith had been under investigation he should not have allowed his name to go forward for election as FCS Chairman. It concluded pointedly:

The committee also feels strongly that all those who aspire to and hold office in the Federation shall, at all times, act with the utmost integrity and responsibility and that their actions at all times should be entirely open and calculated to promote the unity and effectiveness of the Federation as a committee of the National Union.[63]

The committee discovered that Monteith had, 'albeit in good faith', filled in an application form for a student to attend the Federation's conference at Loughborough, but that the student did not belong to the college named. Furthermore, it also discovered that Monteith was not an officer of the Conservative Association concerned and as such the committee concluded:

Notwithstanding the foregoing facts, the committee finds that at Loughborough Mr Monteith was properly elected under the appropriate rules to be

Chairman of the Federation. However, the committee is of the opinion that Mr Monteith was guilty of a grave error of judgment in completing the said application form, particularly as he was already vice-chairman of the Federation, and that he should not have allowed his name to go forward as a candidate for the office of National Chairman of the Federation.[64]

In replying to the report's findings Monteith stated in bullish fashion that it would: 'disappoint many enemies of the Federation, who are faced with defeat in the battle of ideas on the campus'.[65] He argued that the incident over the application form had been a 'miserable, minor point'[66] and said that he had merely recorded information on the form which had been passed to him by telephone. He pointed out that after the student's status had been questioned and reduced from delegate to observer, he had left it to the conference to decide whether his name should go forward for election: 'The conference made the judgment, not me.'[67]

On being elected FCS chairman in early spring 1982, Monteith had tried to get in touch with the Party Chairman, Cecil Parkinson, so as to express concern about the activities of some officials at CCO. Whereas the party was, at this time, being systematically penetrated by increasing numbers of Thatcherite supporters, the FCS's Libertarians viewed the party machinery with grave suspicion. In particular, Monteith and his free market associates distrusted CCO because of its suspected wet 'Heathite' views.[68] While Monteith failed to make contact with Parkinson, because he was at the time a member of the Falklands crisis inner cabinet, this episode serves to illustrate the Libertarians' distrust of CCO. Asked by *The Times* why he had tried to contact the Party Chairman through backbench MPs and not through CCO Monteith replied: 'So that I could be sure of having a private meeting with Cecil Parkinson. I can't say any more than that. You read between the lines, I have still got to work with these guys.'[69]

Monteith was a robust chairman who, during his year of office, led a movement avid to extol ever more radical free market ideas. Peter Young, for instance, still serving on the national committee, wrote a letter to *Times Higher Educational Supplement*, in response to a previous article on the possible privatisation of universities. In it he wrote:

Sir – you write in your editorial of September 24 that 'of course the wholesale privatisation of higher education is unlikely to happen.' I wouldn't be so sure. The tide of ideas is sweeping to the right at such a rate that before long it will even dispose of the debris of our stultified education system. In your hysterical diatribe against the Central Policy Revenue Staff recommendations on education privatization you console yourselves with the thought that 'the civil service with its dedication to the British way will grind such an accumulation of prejudice and ignorance into smaller and smaller pieces until it becomes dust.'

This doesn't seem a terribly democratic approach. I'm sure if the civil service had managed to ditch some silly trendy innovation favoured by the THES, you would be full of righteous indignation. Besides, very soon the civil service will be so small it won't be able to do very much at all. You socialists must simply wake up to the fact that you are on the losing side.[70]

During Monteith's year (1982–83) it was quite clear that the dominant Libertarian faction within FCS went beyond the cosy politics of the post-war consensus. Away from the more traditional battles over NUS, FCS was increasingly seen from outside – and perhaps more importantly began to regard itself – as the Conservative Party's organisation most explicitly engaged in the 'battle of ideas' against Socialism. The issues they dealt with included a radical defence of privatisation in a multitude of areas, many of which were not even being proposed by the Government. Although 1982–83 therefore saw the development of the Libertarian line within FCS, when the 1983 national conference took place, to the surprise of many, the moderate Paul Goodman beat Monteith, who was standing for a second term: 154 votes to 118.[71]

Although the Libertarian faction had dominated the FCS since 1980, in reality this had been achieved only by a broad coalition of radical free marketeers and a small group of nationalists or 'authoritarians' as they were sometimes called. This latter group, which represented populist perceptions of right-wing extremism, broke with the Libertarians and backed Goodman.[72] Contrary to the populist perceptions of the press, throughout the early 1980s the FCS was divided not into two ('Wet' and Libertarian) but three factions. At one end of the political spectrum there were the wets, or moderates, characterised by their belief in the paternalistic principles of a strong welfare state. At the other end were the Libertarians, who based their views solely on the criteria of thwarting the state and a radical advocation of the principles of *laissez-faire* Capitalism. In the middle were the authoritarians, or 'shits', as the Libertarians called them. Not only did they believe in a strong paternalistic state but they were also characterised as being xenophobic racists: they frequently extolled the virtues of such Monday Clubesque values as 'if it's black send it back'.[73]

Although the moderates took over the FCS, it is interesting to note how the definition of moderation had itself changed, especially since the FCS defections to the SDP a mere two years before. The general ideological shift towards the free market meant, for instance, that Goodman and his associates were now in favour of student loans.

In September, at the FCS half-yearly conference, those who took a radical free-market position reasserted their power by blocking a key constitutional change recommended as a safeguard against electoral irregularities. Writing about the power of the Libertarian right at this time David Jobbins of the *Times Higher Education Supplement* wrote:

The conference became chaotic on several occasions, culminating in the unthinkable in Conservative circles – a walkout by some of the delegates as a Government minister was called to speak.

At one stage elements were warned that they would be ejected if they persisted in shouting from the back of the hall.

The moderates won control six months ago but have a tiny majority on the national committee. The right, whose leaders' philosophy is moulded by the virulently anti-interventionist Adam Smith Institute, sensed also that the moderates had only the slimmest of majorities among delegates. They seized every opportunity of demonstrating their ability to challenge what they regarded as a soft line on economic and social policies.

Twice as much time as scheduled was devoted to procedural wrangling over the committee report and only one of ten motions submitted was debated, but voting could not be completed.

The motion, which stood some chance of being passed, would have endorsed the view of Paul Goodman, the Federation's Chairman, that the organisation should build up its activity in the further education colleges and defend the Government's Youth Training Scheme against criticisms from Labour students. In the debate it was clear that many right-wingers distrusted the YTS as an unwarranted intervention in the free market.[74]

Phil Pedley, the notoriously wet chairman of the YCs, and an observer at the conference, accused a 'vociferous minority' of deliberately disrupting the meeting. In a statement to the press he complained:

These people are supposedly Government supporters but the whole tone of their comments is against Government policies. To walk out on a minister shows gross discourtesy and is not going to do the standing of either the FCS of the YCs with the party or Government any good at all.[75]

In January 1984 BBC TV's *Panorama* investigated allegations about links between a number of Conservative Party members and a range of authoritarian far-right groups. On it David Irving claimed that he had bought the mailing list of two thousand FCS members for 'several hundred pounds' from a former chairman. While Goodman said it was not he, and added: 'I do not think selling confidential mailing lists to people like Mr Irving is compatible with membership of the Conservative Party',[76] after a great deal of speculation there followed an emphatic denial from his predecessor, Brian Monteith.[77] To date, nothing has ever been proved regarding these allegations one way or the other.

Overall, Goodman's year as FCS chairman passed relatively un-
eventfully. It was certainly, by comparison with what had gone
before, a quiet year. Not only was there a lot less hostile press coverage, but only one article appeared nationally that articulated any
distinct FCS political campaign message.[78] One month before the
1984 national leadership elections the *Times Higher Education Supplement* reported that Conservative students were again 'planning' to
campaign on the NUS issue:

Conservative students are planning a new assault on what they regard as
non-democratic practices which lead to decisions being unrepresentative of
majority opinion.
 The Federation of Conservative Students this week complained of 'widespread malpractices' despite the steps already taken and called for referen-
dums on important issues, secret ballots and higher quorums at general
meetings.[79]

The April 1984 FCS conference saw the re-emergence of a Libertarian leadership. Although Thatcher praised the moderates, the
membership elected the hard-line Libertarian intellectual Marc-
Henri Glendening as chairman.[80] Without the need for authoritarian
support, the Libertarians made sure that even before their votes were
cast a pro-NUS speech by party chairman John Gummer was jeered
at and heckled.[81]
 The wets had begun the conference with a setback. Salford University's delegation had been excluded at the last moment because of
doubts over their representation, leading in turn to the elimination of
one of their hopefuls for the national committee. Nevertheless, they
were powerful enough to stop a move to have a commitment to
'destroy' the NUS written into the FCS's constitution, and another
effectively to sack Edward Heath as the movement's life patron.
 While Marc-Henri Glendening defeated his opponent, Julian
Samways, by only ten votes, it was clear from the outset that he was
going to be the most outspoken and radical Libertarian leader the
organisation had ever seen. Glendening, born in 1959, had been
from 1976 an active Liberal Party member, serving as their youngest
ever agent during the 1979 election. However, in 1981 he had
switched to the Conservatives and at Warwick University espoused
the politics of the radical free market. Speaking immediately after his
election victory Glendening was quick to challenge Gummer's
authority; he said:

Mr Gummer is entitled to his perspective on student issues, but mine is
rather different ... Mr Gummer's view that we should take over our student
unions and then the NUS has failed. The emphasis of the FCS will now be

on campaigning on issues of a national significance. We believe that working to change NUS is a waste of time.[82]

National Student reported that 'Glendening ... expressed little
interest in NUS'[83] and went on to quote him as saying: 'We will be
still putting a lot of stress on educational issues, grants and loans for
example, but broadening out to look at other, wider issues.'[84]

Marc-Henri Glendening's election marked a watershed in the
FCS's history. For it was under his leadership that the Libertarians
began to apply their paradigm to a broad range of issues including
many which went well beyond the narrow domestic political scene.
Under Glendening, the Federation tabled, for example, five motions
to the 1984 Conservative Party conference, displaying a wide range
of interests. Proposals included: the privatisation of the mining
industry, the breaking of the National Union of Mineworkers
(engaged in their year long national strike), the privatisation of the
National Health Service, and the total integration of Northern Ireland into the rest of the United Kingdom. They also put forward proposals to freeze student grants and to end the NUS closed shop.[85]
Under its new and radical Libertarian management the FCS became
engaged in an unprecedented level of political activity. In August *The
Times* reported an FCS plan to 'picket' a number of London stations
and collect money for working miners whose homes had been damaged by what the Federation abrasively called Scargill's 'Red Fascist
Thugs'.[86] Directly parodying the NUM campaign, FCS hacks stuck
'Smash Scargill' stickers on passing members of the public, and
handed out leaflets demanding the privatisation of the pits. Not used
to this kind of radical activism, *The Times* wondered whether CCO
condoned such 'violence'.[87]

At the 1984 FCS half-yearly conference the Conservative Party
had to overrule an attempt by FCS officers to refuse press credentials
to *National Student* on the basis that they were 'political enemies'. At
this event the wearing of 'Smash Scargill' and Pro-UNITA badges
created some further trouble when it was realised that the Federation
was sharing conference facilities with the Union of Construction and
Allied Technical Trades.[88]

This conference was important because it supported the most radical free market agenda ever seen at an FCS conference. Here resolutions favouring the wholesale privatisation of the universities, the
abolition of the University Grants Committee and the introduction
of a private student loans system (a so-called 'compromise solution'),
under which contracting-in would replace contracting-out of NUS,
became official policy.[89] In continuing their battle with the NUS, the

Federation of Conservative Students co-opted the 'very sound' (ex-FCS) Neil Hamilton MP on to their national committee. Within a month Hamilton was employed to lead a Conservative Student lobby of the House of Commons which urged the immediate introduction of voluntary student union membership.[90]

Opposing state higher education on principle, Glendening attempted to gain the moral high ground by using pseudo-socialist rhetoric. On the issue of student loans he challenged the left by stating:

I don't believe that it will discourage those from a working-class background at all. The present system means that taxes from the working classes are supporting the middle classes where most students came from. Loans would reverse this situation.[91]

After passing, at the 1984 conference, a proposal to abolish by a two-thirds majority the office of Life Patron, albeit subject to ratification in April, Glendening quickly wrote to Edward Heath suggesting he should resign immediately. Glendening complained of his 'persistent attacks' on key government policies and wrote: 'A return of the type of discredited policies associated with your period of office would be a manifest lunacy. Mrs Thatcher has learnt the lesson of history even if you haven't.[92] In reply, Heath wrote:

What we face is a market failure ... I am surprised that a number of your generation have failed to grasp the challenge that confronts us ... I am saddened that you are prepared to acquiesce in the fatalism of the inevitability of unemployment. I am afraid that you commit a gross calumny when you try to equate your own policies to traditional conservatism. To me they seem indistinguishable from the 19th century liberal tradition of unfettered laissez-faire and extreme libertarianism.[93]

There is no doubt that during Glendening's year of office the FCS began to use overtly provocative tactics which represented a break with the Conservative tradition of gentlemanly behaviour. Although it is true that throughout the early 1980s the FCS became progressively more political, in 1984 provocative tactics and disruption became an art form. One unofficial FCS pamphlet called *The Gordon Liddy Guide to Disrupting NUS Conference* stated: 'Always be provocative. Remember, you are not here to persuade the closed-minded leftists. You are here to wind them up so much they lose control and disrupt the conference, eg. 'you red, fascist scum'.[94] Another document that was officially issued regarding the NUS conference, read:

Some will say that we are here to disrupt. This is entirely correct. As long as the NUS forces students into membership the only avenue of protest available is disruption. When the closed shop is broken, and NUS no longer feeds off the taxpayer like a bloated parasite, then the disruption will cease.[95]

At the 1984 NUS conference a number of FCS delegates tried to rush the platform and disrupt proceedings. Guy Roberts, a Conservative student from Leeds University, shouted 'red, fascist scum'[96] in an attempt to halt the NUS committee elections. Another FCS activist delayed proceedings by insisting on a standing order under which the conference would be conducted in Welsh.

Martin Callanan, a member of the FCS national committee, sought to defend these tactics. He said: 'We do not recognise that the NUS has a right to make decisions on our behalf and we have a right to get up and use the ridiculous procedures of the Conference to make our point of view as forcibly as possible.'[97] Although many Conservatives questioned such behaviour, there is evidence that these tactics had the desired effect. NUS president Phil Woolas told Andrew Moncur of the *Guardian*: 'Undoubtedly it causes us damage in just the same way that football hooligans cause damage to Manchester United or wherever.'[98]

To argue however that 1984–85 simply represented the rise of a new group of fanatical 'right-wing extremists' is a misguided oversimplification. 1984–85 was a key year for Conservative students because it witnessed the development of a profound Libertarianism never seen before in the party's youth circles. Although, at the time, few commentators managed to portray this change accurately, one journalist in particular, Andrew Evans of the *Coventry Evening Telegraph*, did so. Swimming against the tide of ignorance in an article entitled 'Beware this fringe group, Tories told',[99] Evans reported that Coventry's Tory leader, Counsellor Arthur Taylor, had warned the city's Conservatives against infiltration by a 'fringe anarchist group'.[100] What was being dealt with here was not a group of authoritarian fascists but instead a group of individualist – or property-rights – anarchists. Dealing mainly with Warwick University's Conservative students, Evans noted the FCS's close relationship with the London-based Libertarian Alliance (LA), an anarcho-capitalist think-tank. On the views of the LA he wrote:

In a leaflet entitled Liberty versus Democracy they say: 'We don't believe in democracy for its own sake. We regard it as just another arrogant monarch … sometimes to be allied with, sometimes to be attacked.' Their statement of aims calls for a 'Sustained intellectual assault on the foundations of statist ideology – whether it be Conservative, fascist, or Socialist.'[101]

Turning to Marc-Henri Glendening the article goes on to quote him as saying:

Libertarianism is capturing the imagination of a growing number of young people in the Conservative Party, at Manchester Poly, at Warwick University, and in the Young Conservatives. [It is] the first really coherent alternative to Marxism and Socialism.[102]

Glendening and his associates were no ordinary group of right-wing extremists. Away from the traditional view of Conservative activism, he not only favoured the international free migration of labour, and radical denationalisation, but is on record for having said: 'I believe in the de-criminalisation of heroin, and all drugs ... I believe that the individual should be responsible for what they want to do to themselves.'[103]

Not surprisingly, pressure began to mount on John Gummer to act over what some were now calling the Conservative Party's 'Militant Tendency'.[104] CCO was reportedly paranoid about the possible spread of Libertarianism into the YCs, and with good reason. It was not long before the most important YC region fell to radical right control. As *The Times* reported:

Right-wingers took control of the Greater London Young Conservatives on Saturday, when an organised group of six, and one like-minded independent, were elected in a clean sweep of senior posts. The winners claimed that their success was a pointer to the ballot now in progress for the national chairmanship and vice-chairmanships of the Young Conservatives, the one prominent section of the Conservative Party still in the hands of the Government's left-wing critics. But the losers said yesterday that the London contest was unlike the national contest, because the winners at Saturday's annual meeting owed much to the organising efforts of far-right elements now in control of the Federation of Conservative Students.[105]

As pressure mounted on Gummer, speculation grew in the press about the FCS's future. For instance, *The Times* reported:

The leadership of the Conservative Party is, for the first time, contemplating drastic action to purge its student body of ultra-right-wing elements which have become an embarrassment to the Prime Minister, and an affront to mainstream Conservatives throughout the country.

The course of events will depend on how next week's annual conference of the Federation of Conservative Students is conducted, and whether intolerant and undemocratic forces prove to have the upper hand.

A growing number of ministers and senior Conservatives, both in Parliament and in the voluntary echelons of the Party, believe that the Federation has become an incurable diseased limb of the National Union, the central voluntary organisation, and will have to be removed.[106]

At the 1985 FCS conference, held at Loughborough University, the Libertarians won another victory with their candidate for chairman Mark MacGregor. Not only was he 'sound' but, as a former chairman of the Scottish FCS (SFCS), he was thought to be experienced in matters of 'high office'. Elected to serve with MacGregor as senior vice-chairman was the Libertarian's foreign-policy guru David Hoile. Another vice chairman elected was the 'Ramboesque' Scottish activist Douglas Smith, so-called on account of his hard-hitting views and tough personality. Commenting on the result *The Times* reported:

Election results published yesterday show that the 14,000-strong body has overwhelmingly voted for officers who espouse many of the controversial right-wing 'libertarian' ideals which have embarrassed the party leadership.

At their most extreme, these ideas include the legalisation of marijuana, heroin and child sex ... Mrs Edwina Currie, one of the most dynamic new Conservative MPs and by no means a 'wet', was defeated in the ballot for vice-president by the more solidly right-wing Mr Neil Hamilton and Mr Alan Howarth.[107]

Although this Conference resulted in an electoral victory for the Libertarians it was a public-relations disaster. According to early Press reports a number of FCS members had caused serious damage to some of the rooms in the university, and as a result John Gummer decided to suspend their £30,000 annual grant immediately.[108] He said: 'I have heard today of actions which took place last night which cannot anywhere or at any time be excused. Damage, hooliganism, and sheer vandalism are totally unacceptable.'[109] Gummer also decided to set up another inquiry into the FCS. This episode was acutely embarrassing for the party, not least because it came only a day after the Prime Minister had widely publicised moves to try to curb soccer hooliganism. Nevertheless, responding to Gummer's decision to cut off funds Mark MacGregor said:

Unfortunately, many of our supporters will see this as a move against the leaders they have elected. Our supporters are from working-class backgrounds, and the party establishment seems to feel that we don't quite fit in.[110]

Similarly, FCS vice-chairman Douglas Smith said: 'They don't like the way we talk, or the way we dress.'[111]

Although the newspapers were full of stories about the FCS's 'rowdy' and extreme behaviour (the story made the front page headline of the *Daily Star*: 'Tory Yobs: College is wrecked in drunken rampage'; and the *Daily Mirror*: 'Tory Louts On The Rampage: Hooray Henries smash rooms at Conference'[112]), after a few days, evidence began to emerge that suggested that Gummer had seriously over-reacted. Although the press had reportedly been informed by CCO staff that over seven hundred cans of beer had been consumed, and that the students had caused many hundreds of pounds' worth of damage, soon serious questions were being asked about what really happened. Under the heading '£14 bill' for Tory Rowdies' Margot Norman of the *Daily Telegraph* wrote:

Damage caused at Loughborough University by delegates to the Federation of Conservative Students' Conference may have been exaggerated ... The University may send the Federation a bill for just £14 ... 'I understand there was no physical damage' said Inspector Patricia Perry yesterday from Loughborough Police Station ... Students cleared up the mess after the offending party, and journalists who saw the room the morning after reported a damaged door handle, a missing light bulb and beer stains on the carpet in a corridor to be the only visible signs of damage.[113]

Similarly, Professor Peter Havard-Williams of Loughborough University wrote, in a letter to *The Times*:

Sir, as warden of the neighbouring hall of residence I heard little of the Conservative Students, unlike many other non-student conferences. There was no rampaging around halls of residence and the damage done was largely, if not solely, in one block. The damage itself was not more than that done by many other conferences and was not excessive.

If senior members of the Conservative Party think that the students' behaviour was exceptional, then they must be widely out of touch with contemporary behaviour in British society – the students were no worse nor better than many of their 'elders and betters'.

One can only conclude that the outburst is further evidence of the present-day politicians' 'student bashing' syndrome. The furore caused raises several questions, including:

1. What was the real motive for John Gummer's precipitate intervention?
2. What were the motives of those who reported the damage in the terms in which they did?[114]

Although it is not possible to determine why Gummer took the action he did, whether or not it was for factional reasons, Sir Alfred Sherman, a policy adviser to Mrs Thatcher, had no doubts. *The Sunday Times* reported:

He is highly critical of John Selwyn Gummer, the Tory Chairman, for sounding off without first discovering the facts but he hints darkly there is more to it than this. 'I am deeply disturbed,' he says 'about the implications of this witch hunt. It's directed against the Prime Minister. The Gummergate affair is not over yet.'[115]

Sherman was right, the Gummergate affair was not over; serious questions persisted. A few days later Toby Young wrote in the *Observer*:

As nights of mob terror go, last Monday's party at the Federation of Conservative Students' Conference was pretty tame ... It is true that the guests included William Tebbit, an FCS activist and son of Norman, and Mike Gould, whose father Sir James Gould is Chairman of the Scottish Conservative Party. But this does not account for the vehemence of the Tory leadership's reaction.[116]

For Young, Gummer's reaction was indeed understandable given the ideological and tactical nature of the FCS. His article went on:

At first sight it might look as if Gummer seriously over-reacted to these pranks, and so caused the Government avoidable embarrassment – especially just after Mrs Thatcher's new plans to cope with football hooligans were announced. In fact, Gummer knew exactly what he was doing. For some time now he has become increasingly worried by the antics of the so-called 'Libertarian' faction of the FCS, and Monday's high jinks furnished the perfect excuse to take their pocket money away.

Obviously these young people, with their bizarre ideas and behaviour, are hoping to shock their elders and betters. But they can't be dismissed quite so easily. For one thing, they have a lot of success in penetrating the more lethargic sections of the party.

For another, their philosophy is uncomfortably close to Mrs Thatcher's. They take the free market economy to its extreme yet logical conclusion. They stretch Victorian values until they snap. They are Thatcherite thinking turned into a 'Spitting Image' puppet.[117]

A few weeks after its announcement, the parameters of the party's inquiry into the FCS changed. Instead of being a 'full investigation into its student wing', the Conservative Party's national executive chairman, Sir Russell Sanderson, wrote to Gummer informing him that the inquiry would now only 'investigate the events at the 1985 Loughborough Conference ... and ... examine whether the organisation ... meets the aims and objectives of the National Union ...'. He went on: 'there is no question of an inquiry into the personal political views of the members of the FCS'.[118] In a clever public relations move, the Federation's leadership quickly invited its vice-president, Alan Howarth MP, to undertake an independent investigation 'in parallel with the inquiry'. Howarth concluded that there had been some 'excesses' at Loughborough, but that in the main early press reports had been 'enormously overblown'. By mid-June speculation was running rife in the press, and amongst right-wing MPs, on whether the FCS had been smeared as part of an anti-Thatcher campaign headed by the leading wet Peter Walker. Martin Fletcher of *The Times* wrote:

For months now, according to the FCS and MPs, Walker has been assiduously wooing those uncommitted MP's – the bulk of the Parliamentary Party – whose votes he must have to win the leadership election when it comes.

The FCS used to be an innocuous organisation espousing moderate policies not too far removed from those of the Young Conservatives. That all changed in 1980. Strident young 'radical Thatcherites' seized control advocating wholesale privatisation, mass delegislation, support for anti-communist 'freedom fighters' ... and the severance of links with the NUS.

At this point the conspiracy theorists come into their own. If the 'wets' cannot retain control of the FCS, runs the line, then they intend to thoroughly discredit it before it begins to send a flow of bright young Thatcherites into Parliament.[119]

When the official party inquiry was delivered it proposed:

> ... a comprehensive review of the federation's rules and constitution to bring it under the full party control nationally and in the regions and stopping the federation from acting as a sovereign body within the party ... [120]

Regarding behaviour at Loughborough, it said:

> As to the conference, there was evidence of partiality on the part of some chairmen, orchestrated responses, an intolerance beyond that expected in the usual cut and thrust of student political debate, and of excessive factionalism leading to acrimonious infighting. [121]

While the report urged radical constitutional changes, none was ever adopted; the National Union dropped its proposals for postal ballots in the election of the FCS's leadership. Instead of reform, it was not long before the Libertarians felt confident enough to remove Edward Heath as FCS Life Patron. Accounting for this lack of action by the party the *Guardian* reported:

> It is understood that Mr Norman Tebbit has enjoyed cordial relations with the FCS since becoming party chairman. Some sources were suggesting yesterday that his replacing Mr Gummer may have been crucial to the turn in the fortunes of the FCS. [122]

Ideologically, these FCS activists were a world away from their predecessors. Instead of the benign and pragmatic Conservatism of the previous generations, they prided themselves on being intellectuals and articulated a wide range of complex and detailed policy ideas, reminiscent of nineteenth-century anarcho-capitalism. [123] Federation members had, for example, addressed the following motion on the denationalization of money at their 1985 conference:

> This Conference believes: The Government monopoly of money must be abolished to stop the recurring bouts of acute inflation and deflation that have become accentuated during the last 60 years. Abolition is also the cure for the more deep-seated disease of the recurring waves of depression and unemployment attributed to 'capitalism'. The monopoly of money by government has relieved it of the need to keep its expenditure within its revenue and thus precipitated the spectacular increase in government expenditure over the last 30 years ... The urgency of competition in currency requires to be demonstrated to the public by a Free Market Movement, comparable to the Free Trade Movement of the 19th Century. [124]

There is no doubt that many in the FCS at this time revelled in their new image of being 'pseudo-Trotskyite' agenda-setting intellectuals. They used their image as a weapon to confound their enemies by going beyond the traditional philosophical matrix of Conservatism and the realities of Adorno. Armed with Anarcho-Capitalist Libertarianism many in FCS believed they were in a better position to out-argue the left: who, it must be said, still talked as if they were up against a group of Fascists. The ideological confidence among FCS members can be clearly seen in this article written by a member of London FCS, about Gummer's £30,000 grant termination:

> Mr Gummer's announcement was the culmination of a more general smear campaign sponsored by Marxists in the National Union of Students aided and abetted by certain wets within the Conservative Party. Incapable of beating FCS through honest, intellectual debate other techniques were used. Those leading the attack were unable to make up their minds whether to accuse the FCS of being Fascist or 'Anarchist!'.[125]

One of the most important developments in the FCS was that of a unified foreign policy. Up until 1984–85, and most importantly the election of David Hoile as vice-chairman, evidence suggests that international relations was a domain largely tied to the politics of 'gung ho nationalism'. However, as Libertarianism took hold judgments became increasingly based on a clear state-versus-market dichotomy. They argued it was logical to combat the forces of state oppression and 'Socialism' because only a market system could protect human rights and sustain prosperity for all. The 'armed struggle' in places like Nicaragua, Angola and Kampuchea was philosophically justified in the ideological terms of a rationality/irrationality conflict. The priority of what the FCS termed 'Freedom Fighters' was to overthrow the most statist regimes first. The problem however, was in the delineation of the boundary of when freedom fighters stop. Ultimately, the FCS – and Libertarians in general – might have found themselves logically supporting any organisation whose purpose was the destabilisation of a state; i.e., Action Directe in France. The strict dichotomy between rationality/irrationality legitimated the FCS's stance on foreign policy issues, for they had furnished themselves with a paradigm that made clear-cut 'Us-and-Them' value judgments. Taking the FCS's Libertarianism to an extreme, anybody who supported any degree of 'statism', was often automatically regarded as a 'Socialist'. The use of such language was particularly successful in the recruitment of new cadres. FCS was both argumentatively hard-hitting and outrageous.

In May 1985 David Hoile outraged many outside the FCS by going on a secret fact-finding mission to Costa Rica, Honduras and Nicaragua.[126] Hoile, the son of a miner who had grown up in Rhodesia, spoke openly to the *Guardian* about his trip. As well as spending eight days on patrol with the Nicaraguan Contras, Hoile told of how he had carried a Kalashnikov, adding: 'it was a very enjoyable experience', and if it had been necessary he would have been 'prepared to use his gun'.[127] The *Guardian* story carried a photograph of Hoile at a Contra camp surrounded by armed soldiers and holding a banner that read: 'FDN-FCS, Fighting for Peace, Freedom and Liberty'. It was adorned with the Conservative Party logo.[128]

By October 1986 many in the higher echelons of the Conservative Party believed that the FCS had become a serious electoral risk that could no longer be tolerated by an organisation dedicated to the winning of elections. For many, the party could not afford to have influential elements within it which acted so outrageously and spoke in the following, anarchic terms:

It is easy for us in FCS, on the 'right' of the political spectrum to forget the enormity of the task which confronts us. It is easy for us to talk of our dogmatic, idealistic approach when we confront the ideologies of the left – they are easy to defeat. Much more difficult is what remains as the prevailing trend within our own Party. Our opponents within the Conservative Party have no ideological stance; they accept expediency as their guide, claiming that the Party has survived by moulding itself to perceived changes in public opinion. Of course they accept certain broad, non ideological principles – respect for the Monarchy, patriotism, law and order etc. But they regard those of us who hold liberty as our highest value as disreputable infiltrators, enemies of the Party who must be smeared and purged.

Expediency had dampened the radicalism and hence impact of Thatcherism. It is our function to perpetuate Thatcherism, to carry forward the crusade in defence of liberty. If the Conservative Party is to become a Party of principle, competing not for the middle, but for the high ground. It is better to remain forever in opposition than to betray our principles and to adopt the policies of Socialism and Fascism. Instead of presenting a mish-mash of policies, we must present a coherent, ideologically based package.[129]

One document that acts as a testimony to the radicalism of the FCS's Libertarians was produced by SFCS in 1986 and distributed at the Scottish Party's National Conference in Perth. The controversial *Manifesto for Scotland* began with the heading 'The First Step' and read: 'In an environment where we wish to promote a liberal economic system, reform must start with the medium that underlines all economic activity, namely money.'[130] It went on:

Since most economists now recognise the relationship between inflation and an increase in the money supply, the perennial problem for successive governments has been the control of the ever-expanding money supply. In practice, Neo-Keynesian policies have proved this better than anything else. Monetarists however, in ignoring the nature of government naively believe that the money supply can be brought under control. To encourage enterprise and development of the type envisaged, what is required is a stable currency attractive to investors, and from which will flow a stability in both supply and prices, and in consequence massive investment, prosperity and jobs. The only way to achieve this is to remove the state's monopoly on the issue and management of currency and replace it with competition between different denominations. This means the complete denationalisation of money by repealing the banking (Scotland) Act 1845 hence empowering new banks to be created and compete within the market.[131]

Continuing down the SFCS's 'Road to Free Enterprise' we find ourselves most definitely presented with policies that can only be described as revolutionary. On welfare:

The Welfare State is costly, inefficient and unmanageable. It should be abolished. Firstly, tax credits would be given to those who contracted out of the NHS and comprehensive education, as compensation for the portion of National Insurance that is paid for these services. Eventually we envisage that there would be no such body as we understand it today. … For less fortunate members of society there would be provision in the form of a voucher system to replace social security … the cost of such a system would be borne by all those who invest in a premium. The NHS would be phased out and replaced by an entirely private system. The education system would ultimately be private at all levels, but as a precursor a system of vouchers would be introduced to carry the individual's allocation of resources. Such a method of capitation funding as opposed to block allocations means that resources are accumulated where there is most demand and hence used more effectively. As the element of competition is introduced, primary and secondary schools and universities and colleges will compete with each other, leaving the better institutions to flourish and expand, and the poorer ones to disappear.

On freeports and freezones:

… we wish to see deregulation in the areas of labour relations, planning controls and business law and order to harness the energy of small, voluntary groups and small enterprise. This would lead to the creation of Freeports and Freezones at Leith, Aberdeen, Dundee and Glasgow.

On housing:

In keeping with the ideal of a mobile, property-owing democracy, all council stock must be available for sale, this function being tendered out to private, commercial estate agents. With respect to empty public property or such that is difficult to let, the option should be open to sell such land and buildings for private development. In all events the tenants should possess as of right, the ability to force the purchase of such stock.

On the denationalisation of roads:

Investment will be drawn from the private sector to fund construction of roads such as turning the A74 into a motorway. The return can be likened to a dividend and will be commensurable with usage. At the inception of such a network, usage would be measured by a system of hidden cables and electronic counting. Once the whole of Britain was covered this would be done by an Automatic Vehicle Identification System (AVI) that works on the principle of bar coding. At the same time Vehicle Excise Duty would be abolished.

On prison management:

A far-sighted politician recently noted that Barlinnie, Saughton and Peter-head could be 'better run by Reo Stakis, Trust House Forte and Thistle Hotels'. Not unnaturally the less enlightened in the Party convulsed and promptly dissociated themselves from such a view. The sad fact is that this view is accurate ... Why not franchise out this function to Group 4 Security or Securicor?

On BBC Scotland:

The TV licence should be abolished as it is unfair on the viewer who watches little BBC television in the same way that the Vehicle Excise Duty is on persons who do not use their car as frequently as others. The flat-rate inequality assumes that everyone who watches BBC TV gains the same ben-efit and satisfaction. The operation should be funded like the IBA ... Radio Stations will be split off and sold.

On prostitution:

Another measure that would go far to reducing the incidence of sex crime is the removal of prostitution as one of society's taboos through decriminali-sation, thereby creating a market open to all ... With respect to immorality, the choice is ultimately for the individual to make in exercising one's liberty. It is not a function of the law to dictate what is morally good for the indi-vidual. As for health dangers, in a market where only the best will succeed, it will be in the interests of the ladies or gentlemen involved, to retain a clean bill of health, possibly through a trade association or guild.

On euthanasia:

The freedom to die is the ultimate freedom of any individual and at present it is being denied ... When people reach such a state and wish to die this should not be denied, for it is a fundamental right.

On surrogate motherhood:

The sanctity of life, the benefits and practicalities of 'womb leasing' and the issues of individual right are ignored by empty and hypocritical 'moral' protestations ... By opening a 'market for motherhood' everybody wins. The pregnant woman gains financially, the baby is provided with a loving home, and a married couple are provided with a child of their own ... More-over, such a market would do away with the bureaucratic inadequacies of the present, unjust system of central planning, of adoption and foster care.[132]

These policy proposals, included in a twenty-four page report, illustrate the FCS's Libertarian beliefs. Dealing with many more issues than has been mentioned here – including: mining, north sea oil, British Gas, the Post Office, British Railways, land tenure, indus-trial relations, media reportage, and incest – the case was made that individuals should be allowed to control and socio-economically regulate their own lives. The fundamental view was expressed that, if set free, individuals would be better-placed to achieve a much higher standard of living than under the present system of taxation and state control.

Like their Scottish colleagues, London Conservative Students (LCS) also began to publish material that could not be called 'Conservative' or 'authoritarian' by any traditional standards. In an article which appeared in LCS's *New Agenda* magazine, Edward Pearce openly criticised the Royal Family, an unprecedented move in Conservative Party circles. He asserted:

> ... The market for pure razzle which delights loyal cockneys and people with the political reflexes of Noel Coward, is not what it was; and if the Palace is smart it will understand as much. The decades of sequined fraudulence which made dumb women open their mouths and say 'ahh' are very nearly over.[133]

The final blow to the FCS came in the latter part of 1986, when the Conservative Party decided to close it down. In August *New Agenda* published an article accusing Harold Macmillan of being a war criminal. In the form of an interview with Count Nicholas Tolstoy, it claimed that there could be 'no element of doubt' that the former Prime Minister had given orders, whilst Minister Resident in Italy during 1945, which resulted in 40,000 captured Cossacks being sent to their deaths at the hands of the Soviets after the war.[134] Offering Macmillan a right to reply, the magazine's editor, Harry Phibbs, went on to say: 'If he fails to accept the offer the Conservative Whip should be withdrawn from him in the House of Lords as the Conservative Party should not be associated with War Criminals in any way.'[135] Calling this a 'disgraceful attack on a distinguished former Prime Minister',[136] Party Chairman Norman Tebbit immediately complained that the article had been 'published without being referred to anybody in authority at Conservative Central Office. Had that happened such an article would never have been sanctioned by anyone in authority in the Conservative Party.'[137]

Phibbs was no stranger to controversy. One of the more vocal and militant of young Conservative ideologues, he had previously gained massive press coverage whilst a pupil at school for having been arrested by the KGB at Moscow Airport for attempting to smuggle multilateral disarmament leaflets.[138]

Attempting to defuse the storm created by the article, the new FCS chairman, John Bercow, sided with the party. He stated:

> Regardless of the content of the interview in question, on which people may hold different views, the fact is Harry didn't follow the proper procedures. He is making much of this being a matter of principle but he cannot do that while cowering behind the FCS imprint.[139]

Although Bercow publicly dissociated himself from the article, the fact is that up until that point a great deal of FCS literature had been passed without CCO approval. Bercow was clearly trying to placate the party and thereby secure a future for the now gravely threatened FCS.[140] Before an emergency meeting of the its national committee he threatened to censure Phibbs. However, opinions differed widely as how best to react to the situation and many Libertarians soon made it clear that they supported Phibbs in his battle against the party's establishment. Many predicted an 'almighty row and a deep split'.[141] In an attempt to deter the party from being too hard on Phibbs the Libertarians decided to launch an ambitious programme of political activity. They calculated that a full diary would somehow protect them from closure. As SFCS members announced their intention to be present at a Unionist rally in East Belfast's Shankhill Road,[142] and thus show solidarity in the struggle against 'Marxist terrorism', David Hoile announced the departure of eleven FCS activists to a training course at Washington's Heritage Foundation.[143] Although these political hawks wanted to deter the party from taking further action, this programme of events no doubt caused, as the *Guardian*, put it: '... still further dismay to more cautious elements of the Party Leadership'.[144]

In seemingly bullish mood, the hardliners continued their campaign. One national committee member went so far as to say:

It seems to be the case that if Phibbs gets the chop all will be well; otherwise, the FCS is on the line ... But all that would do would inconvenience us for a while: you can kill the structure but not the spirit. We'd just move en masse into the Young Conservatives.

All this stuff about Macmillan is just schmaltz. He's a former Prime Minister and an old guy, but he was responsible for many of the sufferings which the British people endure today.[145]

Although Phibbs resigned shortly after from the FCS national committee, there is no doubt that for many Libertarians involved the issue was not Stockton's war record, but instead his brand of Conservatism. Many saw the episode as a part of the battle against the wets who were personified by Macmillan's period of 'Socialist domination'.

In October 1986 Norman Tebbit announced the reorganisation of the Party's student wing and the FCS was no more.[146] As we later see in Chapter IV, while the structure had been killed, the spirit lived on and grew. However, before analysing how Libertarianism prospered and developed beyond the Party's student wing, entering both the YCs and the NACG, it is important first to examine the precise nature of the FCS's spirit and its ideologically based anarchic culture.

Notes and References

1. See: Abrams, P. and Little, A., 'The Young Activist in British Politics', *British Journal of Sociology*, Vol. XVI., No. 4, (1965) p. 317.
2. Ibid., pp. 316–17.
3. Ibid., p. 317.
4. Ibid.
5. Ibid.
6. Ibid., p. 310.
7. Ibid., p. 319.
8. Ibid.
9. Ibid., p. 331.
10. John Buchan was also the author of *The Thirty–Nine Steps*. He was later made the 1st Baron Tweedsmuir.
11. David Hoile in a recorded interview with the author, late 1987.
12. Levitas, R., (1986) 'Tory Students and the New Right', *Youth and Policy*, No. 16, p. 2.
13. *T.H.E.S.*, 5 April 1974.
14. See: Levitas, R., 'Tory Students', p. 2.
15. *T.H.E.S.*, 4 March 1977.
16. See: Levitas, R., 'Tory Students', p. 2.
17. Ibid.
18. Quoted in *The Times*, 6 April 1977.
19. See: Levitas, R., 'Tory Students', p. 2. Also see: Butt, R., 'What will the new Tories of Ashfield think of this Dogma gone mad?', *The Times*, 5 May 1977.
20. Levitas, R., 'Tory Students', pp. 2–3.
21. *The Times*, 1 February 1978.
22. Ibid.
23. See: Levitas, R., 'Tory Students', p. 3.
24. Ibid.
25. Ibid.
26. *The Times*, 11 April 1978.
27. Ibid.
28. Quoted in *T.H.E.S.*, 20 October 1978.
29. *The Times*, 10 December 1979.
30. *The Times*, 9 January 1980; *The Times*, 10 January 1980; *T.H.E.S.*, 21 March 1980.
31. *T.H.E.S.* April 1980, p. 3.
32. Ibid.
33. Ibid.
34. Levitas, R., 'Tory Students', p. 3.
35. *T.H.E.S.*, 1 2 September 1980, p. 28.
36. *The Times*, 25 October 1980, p. 3.
37. Ibid.
38. Ibid.
39. *T.H.E.S.*, p. 2.
40. Ibid. Regarding student loans also see: *T.H.E.S.*, 7 November 1980, p. 2; *T.E.S.*, 7 Novemmber 1980, p. 6.
41. *T.H.E.S.*, 24 April 1981.
42. Ibid.
43. *The Times*, 12 August 1981, p. 1.
44. Ibid. Also see: *The Times*, 13 August 1981, p. 2.
45. *The Times*, 13 August 1981, p. 9.
46. As became clear in a series of recorded interviews with the author, there was a high level of hostility between the factions which was frequently expressed through the use of such language.
47. *T.H.E.S.*, 21 August 1981, p. 2.

48. Ibid.
49. Ibid.
50. Ibid.
51. Ibid.
52. *T.H.E.S.*, 8 August 1981, p. 4.
53. *T.H.E.S.*, 1 September 1981, p. 4.
54. *T.E.S.*, 5 September 1981, p. 6. Also see *T.H.E.S.*, 2 October 1981, p. 5.
55. *Guardian*, 2 April 1982, p. 2.
56. Ibid.
57. *T.H.E.S.*, 9 April 1982, p. 4.
58. *T.H.E.S.*, 6 April 1982, p. 4. Also see: *T.H.E.S.*, 30 April 1982.
59. *Guardian*, 27 April 1982, p. 7.
60. Levitas, R., 'Tory Students', p. 4.
61. Ibid. See also: National Union of Conservative and Unionist Associations, (1981) *Report of the Committee of Inquiry concerning the Federation of Conservative Students*, pp. 3–6.
62. Ibid.
63. *The Times*, 9 July 1982, p. 2. Also see: *Guardian*, 9 July 1982; back page; *The Times*, 10 July 1982, p. 2; *T.H.E.S.*, 16 July 1982, p. 4; *The Times*, 23 July 1982, p. 2; *T.H.E.S.*, 30 July 1982, p. 23; *Searchlight*, August 1982; *T.H.E.S.*, 3 September 1982, p. 3.
64. *The Times*, 9 July 1982, p. 2.
65. Ibid.
66. *The Times*, 10 July 1982, p. 2.
67. Ibid.
68. The term 'Heathite wets' was commonly used by Libertarians to describe the staff at CCO. A subtle indication of their mistrust of CCO can be found in *The Times*, 10 July 82, p. 2.
69. Ibid.
70. Letter by Peter Young in *T.H.E.S.*, 8 October 82, p. 31.
71. *T.H.E.S.*, 1 April 83, p. 4.
72. *T.H.E.S.*, 24 February 84, p. 4.
73. According to Zig Layton-Henry, during the Ugandan refugee crisis of the 1973: '… there appeared to be increasing cooperation between members of the Monday Club and the National Front, and it appeared that in some cases this was due to National Front infiltration of Club branches. At the Monday Club rally on 16 September in the Central Hall, Westminster, there was ample evidence of National Front participation. At the Uxbridge by-election in December the West Middlesex branch of the Monday Club was dissolved for endorsing the National Front candidate.' See: Layton-Henry, Z., (1980) *Conservative Party Politics*, Basingstoke, Macmillan, p. 66.
74. *T.H.E.S.*, 16 September 83, p. 5.
75. Ibid.
76. *T.H.E.S.*, 3 February 84, p. 3.
77. Ibid.
78. *T.H.E.S.*, 24 February 84, p. 4.
79. Ibid.
80. Levitas, R., 'Tory Students', p. 4.
81. Ibid. Also see: *National Student*, April, 1984.
82. *National Student*, 16 April 84.
83. Ibid.
84. Ibid.
85. Levitas, R., 'Tory Students', p. 5.
86. *The Times*, 17 August 84, p. 8.
87. Ibid. Also see: Levitas, R., 'Tory Students', p. 5.
88. Levitas, R., 'Tory Students'.

89. Ibid. Also see: *T.H.E.S.*, 7 September 1984, p. 7.
90. Levitas, R., 'Tory Students', p. 5. Also see: *T.H.E.S.*, 21 December 84, p. 4.
91. Glendening quoted in *National Student*, 19 April 1984, p. 2.
92. *The Times*, 3 December 84, p. 12. Also see: *T.H.E.S.*, 7 December 84, p. 9; *T.H.E.S.*, 11 January 85, p. 5; *The Times*, 14 January 85, p. 2; *Sunday Times*, 3 February 85; *The Times*, 27 February 85, p. 10.
93. Edward Heath quoted in *The Times*, 7 January 85, p. 14.
94. FCS (1984) 'Campaign to Smash the Red Menace', *The Gordon Liddy Guide to Disrupting NUS Conference*, p. 2. Gordon Liddy was a member of the CIA's 'dirty tricks' department and involved in Watergate.
95. See: Levitas, R., 'Tory Students', p. 5.
96. *Guardian*, 10.12.84, p. 1.
97. Ibid.
98. *Guardian*, 10 December 84, p. 15.
99. *Coventry Evening Telegraph*, 15 August 84.
100. Ibid.
101. Ibid.
102. Ibid.
103. See: Levitas, R., 'Tory Students', p. 5.
104. It was around this time, as the Militant Tendency began to exercise power within the Labour Party, that many within the Conservative Party began to think of the FCS in Militant terms. See, for example: *T.E.S.*, 12 April 85.
105. *The Times*, 25 February 85, p. 5.
106. *The Times*, 30 March 85.
107. *The Times*, 4 April 85.
108. *Daily Telegraph*, 4 April 85.
109. Ibid.
110. *The Times*, 4 April 1985.
111. Ibid.
112. *Daily Star*, 3 April 1985, p. 1; *Daily Mirror*, 3 April 1985, p. 1.
113. *Daily Telegraph*, 6 April 1985.
114. Letter to *The Times*, 12 April 1985, p. 15.
115. *Sunday Times*, 14 April 1985, p. 16.
116. *Observer*, 7 April 1985.
117. Ibid. For more about Loughborough see: *Guardian*, 4 April 85; *Daily Telegraph*, 4 April 85, p. 1; *T.E.S.*, 5 April 85, p. 3; *T.H.E.S.*, 5 April 85, p. 3; *The Times*, 13 April 85, p. 2; *Daily Telegraph*, 6 April 85; *Sunday Telegraph*, 7 April 85; *Sunday Times*, 7 April 85, p. 2; *Daily Telegraph*, 10 April 85; *Daily Telegraph*, 11 April 85; *T.H.E.S.*, 12 April 85, p. 4; *T.E.S.*, 12 April 85, p. 3; *The Times*, 16 April 85, p. 2; *T.H.E.S.*, 19 April 85, p. 1; *Private Eye*, 19 April 85; *T.E.S.* 19 April 85, p. 3; *The Times*, 26 April 85, p. 1; *National Student*, Late April 1985, p. 3; *The Times*, Diary, 2 May 85, p. 12; *Private Eye*, 03.05.85; *T.H.E.S.*, 3 May 85, p. 3; *The Times*, 7 June 85, p. 2; *The Times*, 6 December 85; *The Times*, 14 December 85, p. 2; *T.E.S.*, 21 June 85, p. 14; *T.H.E.S.*, 13 September 85, p. 1.
118. *National Student*, Early May 1985.
119. *The Times*, 12 June 85.
120. *The Times*, 14 June 85, p. 2.
121. Ibid.
122. *Guardian*, 15.11.85.
123. See: Martin, J. J., (1970) *Men Against the State: The Expositors of Individualist Anarchism in America 1827–1908*, Colorado Springs, Ralph Myles Publisher. Also see: Warren, J., (1846) *Equitable Commerce*, self published, New Harmony; Warren, J., (1863) *True Civilization*, self published, Boston. Tucker, B., (1893) *Instead of a Book*, self published, New York.
124. Federation of Conservative Students, (1985) Economic Policy, *Motions to Conference*, Amendment Four, p. 15. Also see: Dowd, K., (1988) *Private Money*, Hobart

Paper No. 112, London, Institute of Economic Affairs. Hayek, F. A. (1978) *Denationalisation of Money: The Argument Refined*, Hobart Paper No. 70, London, Institute of Economic Affairs. Hayek, F. A. (1978) *New Studies in Philosophy, Politics and Economics*, London, Routledge & Kegan Paul, Part 4, Chapter 13, pp. 218–31. Clarke, A., (1992) *The Micropolitics of Free Market Money: A Proposal*, Economic Notes No. 39, London, Libertarian Alliance.

125. Federation of Conservative Students (London Region), (Autumn 1985) *New Agenda*, Vol. 1, No. 1, p. 5.
126. See: *Guardian*, 9 July 1985.
127. Ibid. Also see: Time Out, 11 July 1985; *T.H.E.S.*, 19 July 1985, p. 6.
128. See: *Guardian*, 9 July 1985.
129. Anonymous, (1986) *Armageddon*, 3 Chester Street, Edinburgh, SCCO, p. 9.
130. Scottish Federation of Conservative Students, (May, 1986) *A Conservative Manifesto for Scotland*, 3 Chester Street, Edinburgh, SCCO, p. 6.
131. Ibid.
132. Ibid., pp. 8–24.
133. Pearce, E., 'Royalty For Grown-ups', in Phibbs, H., (ed.) *New Agenda*, Federation of Conservative Students (London Region), Vol. 1, No. 2, Winter 1985–1986, p. 31.
134. See: *Daily Telegraph*, 19 August 1986, pp. 1–2; *The Times*, 19 June 1986; *The Times*, 20 August 1986, p. 10; *The Times*, 20 August 1986, *Editorial; Daily Telegraph*, 20 August 1986, p. 17; *Guardian*, 20 August 1986; *Guardian*, 21 August 1986., Back Page; *The Times*, 21 August 1986, p. 1; *Guardian*, 21 August 1986; *The Times*, 22 August 1986, p. 1; *Guardian*, 22 August 1986, p. 1; *Sunday Times*, 24 August 1986, p. 3; *Sunday Times*, 24 August 1986, p. 28; *Guardian*, 25 August 1986, p. 1; *T.H.E.S.*, 5 September 1986; *Portsmouth News*, 8 September 1986; *Guardian*, 8 September 1986, p. 5; *The Times*, 19 September 1986, p. 1; *The Times*, 9 October 1986, p. 16; *The Times*, 25 November 1986, p. 16; *The Times*, Diary, 26 November 1986, p. 16.
135. See: *Daily Telegraph*, 19 August 1986, p. 1.
136. Ibid.
137. Ibid.
138. Ibid., p. 2. Also see: *Daily Telegraph*, 20 August 1986, p. 17.
139. *The Times*, 20 August 1986, p. 1.
140. See: *Guardian*, 20 August 1986; *T.H.E.S.*, 5 September 1986; *The Times*, 19 September 1986, p. 1.
141. *Guardian*, 20 August 1986.
142. Ibid.
143. Ibid.
144. Ibid.
145. Ibid.
146. See: *The Times*, 12 December 1986, p. 2; *The Times*, 23 December 1986, p. 12; *Guardian*, 27 December 1986.

Chapter III

THE RISE OF THE YOUNG LIBERTARIAN RIGHT AND PSEUDO-LEFTIST EMULATION

This chapter traces the emergence of Libertarian thought within the FCS back to St Andrews University, and goes on to examine the movement's subsequent culture and politics. It links the attitudes, beliefs and behaviour of the Federation's Libertarian faction with an analysis of both their intellectual roots and their iconography. It concentrates on how the Conservative Party's young Libertarian right was influenced by a variety of free market authors, academics and pressure groups, and how their ideas related to the creation of a distinctly anarchistic political world-view.

3.1 The Role and Importance of the St Andrews Set

While it is always difficult to explain historical events and the precise nature of the relationship between individuals, their ideas and wider social factors such as class, there is little doubt that the St Andrews University Conservative Association had a major determining influence on the political orientation of the FCS in the 1970s. For St Andrews University was the place where a number of Conservative students gathered – seemingly by accident – who were to play a leading role in the subsequent rise of Libertarianism within the Federation. Although there were others, for instance at the London School of Economics, St Andrews emerged as the main staging post, the cat-

---

Notes for this section begin on page 74.

alyst, for the FCS's Libertarian 'first wave'.[1] Michael Forsyth, Bob Dunn and Michael Fallon (to name but a few) all went there. Later to become MPs, they were important figures in the early development of such esoteric ideas as privatisation and deregulation. As mentioned in Chapter II, Forsyth became the first Libertarian chairman of the FCS, and later chairman of the entire Conservative Party in Scotland.[2] At the heart of the St Andrews set however, was Madsen Pirie, who was once described as 'a sort of right-wing Trotsky'.[3] Pirie, along with his former St Andrews colleague Eamonn Butler, set up the influential Adam Smith Institute (ASI) in 1977 and from there influenced many newcomers to the FCS.

Pirie and the St Andrews set made a major impact on British politics under Mrs Thatcher[4] and to this day remain very proud of their achievements. Pirie more recently wrote in an article entitled 'The Cross of St Andrews':

> The University of St Andrews Conservative Association has made an extraordinary contribution to British life. Its members began and sustained an intellectual contribution to policy debate which has had a profound effect on the movement of ideas. Those ideas have helped to transform Britain, and through their success at home, have seen their influence spread around the world.
>
> In the 1960s and 1970s university students generally tended to the political left. In St Andrews, a large number of them espoused the then unfashionable ideas of the free market. At a time when other universities were gaining reputations for student violence or intolerance, a St Andrews group was steadily developing policy ideas to transfer decision making power away from bureaucrats and planners, and into the hands of individual consumers.
>
> Familiar ideas such as privatization, the discounted sale of council houses, floating exchange rates and market led solutions were hammered out in the North Street Bar, the Union Bar, or in the corridors of Sallies or John Burnet Hall. They were honed during innumerable late pier walks, and discussed in the pages of Conservative Association magazines and newsletters.[5]

Dealing specifically with the nature and importance of the St Andrews activists, Pirie went on:

> The group effectively constituted a University within the University. It directed a learning experience. New students would join and take part in the process, while older ones moved on. Those who passed through are now to be found in various walks of life. Six are in Parliament, two as ministers. Two run the Adam Smith Institute. Others are to be found in other Think Tanks, in the universities, in the Bank of England. All were influenced by their experiences at university.
>
> When there have been distinctive movements at other universities invariably there have been members of staff who fed them and kept

them going. A curious feature of the St Andrews Conservatives was that it was always a student affair. The Modern History Professor, Norman Gash, and his wife lent a benign patronage to the Conservative students without necessarily sharing their views or their almost missionary zeal.[6]

In 1971 members of the St Andrews University Conservative Association distributed a spoof 1981 *Daily Telegraph* at their annual conference. It contained many of their political dreams and amongst other things spoke of such policies as council house sales and the privatisation of the telephone service under the name 'Telecom'. Regarding its prophetic nature, Pirie has recently said:

> Uncannily, among its predictions was the election of Ronald Reagan as US President nine years later. Not all of its forecasts were as accurate. We have yet to witness the sale of the Post Office as 'Speedipost', or the incorporation of The Guardian into the Daily Telegraph.[7]

Conservative students at St Andrews constituted an élite group of intellectuals who not only shared a new set of exciting policy ideas, but carried with them a deep sense of fighting against the odds. As this following extract indicates, the FCS tradition of being outrageous and hard-hitting was not simply the preserve of the FCS's 'second wave' (1980–86). Such tactics were also used – although admittedly in not such an extreme manner – by the pioneers of its 'first wave'. For Pirie:

> The established views of the time were hostile, which gave the St Andrews students the status of underdogs. Their activities were characterised by a huge sense of fun, considerable style, and a fair amount of mischief. A Christmas collection bought stereo equipment for the troops in Northern Ireland. One annual dinner was the subject of a left-wing protest, with demonstrators booked in from all over Britain. The Conservative Association held it a week ahead of the announced date. A demonstration planned against another meeting was thwarted because none of the announcements revealed its location. Six protesters eventually found it, too late, at the Crow's Nest in Anstruther.
>
> Trivial incidents such as these added laughter to every day. The heady mixture of bright ideas and enormous fun imparted, to many of the group, a lasting affection for the experience and the place where they shared it. When Britain looked from the disillusion and failure of the 1970s with their corporatism and centralism, it found a coherent and developed alternative. Ideas and policies nurtured in St Andrews have proved their worth.[8]

If any group is to be accorded the title of being the forbearers of Libertarian youth politics in Britain, then it must be the Conservative students of St Andrews. They not only set the intellectual and ideological tone for the FCS in the years that followed, but they had a major impact upon the style of activism adopted.[9]

3.2 The Intellectualisation of Conservative Youth Structures: the Nature, Role and Importance of the Libertarian Paradigm

The FCS's Libertarianism rested upon a complex – but unified – belief system that encompassed values and an *esprit de corps* not easily discernible to outside observers. Because it imbibed many esoteric views and codes of behaviour, the movement's actions, ethos, and iconography can only be really understood after the authors and ideas which influenced it have been fully examined.

Friedrich Hayek's *The Road to Serfdom* [10] was written in 1944 and influenced an increasing number of FCS activists from the late 1960s onwards. A reaction against the collectivist principles of the Nazis (from which he was a refugee), it argued that as a result of their centralised state, Fascism and Socialism led to a parallel totalitarianism. Hayek argued that any system that relied upon heavy interventionist policies led in the long run to inefficiency, unemployment and widespread social decay. However, in the cosy and consensual postwar world of nationalisation, free school milk and Keynesian economics his ideas were marginalised and ignored.

In 1922, Hayek had encountered the 'Austrian School of Economics' under Professor Ludwig Von Mises. Profoundly affected by his anti-socialist teachings, Hayek spent much of the rest of his life exploring the truth of this school's ideas. The Austrian School sees society as a web of complex human interactions, in which prices act as signals for human behaviour:

> For the 'Austrian economist' the free market and the language of price are the very sources and mechanisms of wealth, the diversity of goods produced by many individuals is richer and more useful, ensuring greater and more widespread wealth than any system which attempts to control from the centre. A diversity of different attempts to predict future needs is what guarantees innovation. The role of market pricing is partly that of allocating resources to the preferred use. Its more important role however, is that of transmitting information about preferences and about relative scarcities. Only markets can effectively utilise information dispersed throughout millions of economic agents. Profit is a signal which demonstrates that the entrepreneur is doing the right thing for people he cannot know. Price is therefore the language of the complex or extended order of modern societies. The knowledge utilised in this extended order is greater than that which any single agent such as a government department can possibly acquire. [11]

Hayek's (Austrian) theory has three fundamental strands: the primacy of individual freedom, the value of the market mechanism, and the assertion that the goal of 'social justice' is not only fruitless (because there is no such thing) but actively harmful, because it can and will (so he argues) end up by destroying individual freedom. Hayek offers Libertarian students an accessible and useful definition of freedom which can be narrowly defined as the 'absence of state coercion or restraint'. It embraces political liberty, free speech and economic freedom (coercion itself is only defined in strictly limited cases, such as the protection of 'individual liberty' or 'property'). These coherent and easily accessible definitions offered the FCS 'intellectual ammunition' against Marxists which had not been available given traditional Conservative thought. When it came to attacking the Marxist hegemony on campus Hayek was found to be better than Quintin Hogg.

For Hayek, the market has been historically beneficial to humanity, because it is efficient, and protects individual choice and freedom:

> [It is] a procedure which has greatly improved the chances of all to have their wants satisfied. It is the only procedure yet discovered in which information widely dispersed among millions of men can be effectively utilised for the benefit of all – and used by assuring to all an individual liberty desirable on ethical grounds.[12]

Hayek stated comprehensively the superiority of the market to provide for the 'needs of all' and in so doing provided the FCS with simple arguments against the 'obvious' merits of the social-justice paradigm.

Questions surrounding the issues of social justice and ethics have been given more attention since the mid-1970s. With the revival of political philosophy, Robert Nozick advanced from Hayek's basic position to argue that everyone should have the right to distribute, as they see fit, the rewards of their own labour.[13] He called this principle, 'Justice in Holdings' and it had three elements. A person should be entitled to a holding if he or she has acquired it:

(a) through earnings – 'justice in acquisition'; or
(b) through the inheritance of wealth which was justly acquired – 'justice in transfer'.
(c) Holdings that fall under neither of these categories cannot be justified, hence the government may redistribute holdings acquired illegally – 'the principle of rectification'.

Nozick regards taxation to be theft since it removes from individuals legitimately acquired capital they would have otherwise allocated. Moreover, taxation is suggested to be feudal because it amounts to a form of slavery. By being coerced to spend a considerable part of time working for the state and its agents, taxpayers are *de facto* serfs.

Such arguments enabled Conservative students to challenge the left, for when they argued that Britain was a Capitalist society, and that its ills were the product of the free market, the FCS could reply that it was a mixed economy with large elements of state control and that its ills were the product of 'Socialism'. Armed with Libertarianism, the homeless of London were not the result of Britain's capitalism, or 'Thatcherism', but instead the consequence of state rules and regulations which preclude the operation of a genuine free market in housing. Such poverty is the result of the tax system imposed on rented property, the various Rent Acts with their complex rules, and the Government's restrictions on building in the Green Belt.

While exponents of the free market, from Adam Smith to Friedrich Hayek, defended capitalism on the basis of its overall social product and its capacity to create wealth for the benefit of all, the American philosopher and novelist Ayn Rand provided the FCS with a moral, ethical and epistomological defence of capitalism. For Rand:

> The moral justification of capitalism does not lie in the altruist claim that it represents the best way to achieve 'the common good' ... the moral justification of capitalism lies in the fact that it is the only system consonant with man's rational nature, that it protects man's survival *qua* man, and that its ruling principle is: Justice.[14]

One of the unique features of Rand's defence of capitalism is, as Douglas J. Den Uyl and Douglas B. Rasmussen have argued, that it neither considers capitalism a necessary evil (as do many Conservatives), nor does she attempt to defend it in terms of ends (as do many economists). Instead, the essence of capitalism is individual rights: if individual rights are respected, then that society is capitalist. To understand Rand's theory of rights one must not only grasp her ethical doctrine, but also her fundamental philosophy of man.

Based on an essentially Aristotelian model of human action, Rand's conception of man emphasises the creative power of the human mind. The degree to which one's knowledge increases is argued to be a function of one's ability effectively to solve problems. Against the claims of determinism and the purveyors of over-socialised models of human action, Rand argues there is no static set of rules that if followed will lead automatically to new insights into a given problem. In both her fictional and non-fictional works the creative mind is identified as the dynamic, inspirational force behind all human progress: 'Men of genius in both the sciences and the arts are those who do not allow themselves to be held down by received wisdom.'[15]

Under Rand's philosophy, which she called Objectivism, because of its Aristotelian-realist epistemological and metaphysical views on objective reality, the fundamental alternative facing living things is productive or destructive action. In the case of human beings, those courses of action necessary for the furtherance of our existence are not automatically determined, but chosen. Because we have no automatic means for the furtherance of our lives, we are forced to make choices about which course(s) of action to take. Therefore, the volitional nature of Man's consciousness implies *a priori* a principle of freedom. To act as if there is some substitute for this volitional feature of human nature is to contradict a fundamental metaphysical fact about our nature. Capitalism is not merely 'a social system based on the recognition of individual rights',[16] but more importantly, 'it is the basic, metaphysical fact of man's nature – the connection between his survival and his use of reason – that capitalism recognises and protects'.[17]

Rand defines reason as the ability to conceptualise material provided by the senses. She argues that our very survival requires that we conceptually attend to the empirical world. Ultimately, human choice rests upon whether to direct our full attention to the situations we experience or to base perception on whim; the universe according to Rand being intelligible and potentially understandable.

In *For the New Intellectual* she uses two philosophical ideal types to depict the enemies of rationality and therefore capitalism; the Witch Doctor and Attila:

> The essential characteristic of these two remain the same in all ages: Attila, the man who rules by brute force, acts on the rage of the moment, is concerned with nothing but the physical reality immediately before him, respects nothing but man's muscles, and regards a fist, a club or a gun as the only answer to any problem ... [18]

The Witch Doctor, or the Kantian philosopher, wishes to avoid empirical evidence and the world of demonstrable reality:

> [He is] the man who dreads physical reality, dreads the necessity of practical action, and escapes into his emotions, into visions of some practical realm where he wishes to enjoy a supernatural power unlimited by the absolute of nature.[19]

For Rand, both the Witch Doctor and Attila exist with a 'consciousness held down to the perceptual method of functioning, an awareness that does not choose to extend beyond the automatic, the immediate, the given, the involuntary, which means: an animal's epistemology, or as near to it as a human consciousness can come.'[20]

> It is against the faculty of reason that Attila and the Witch Doctor rebel. The key to both their souls is the longing for the effortless, irresponsible, automatic consciousness of an animal. Both dread the necessity, the risk and the responsibility of rational cognition. Both dread the fact that 'nature, to be commanded, must be obeyed.' Both seek to exist, not by conquering nature, but by adjusting to the given, the immediate, the known.[21]

Armed with Rand, you know who your enemies are. Applying her ideas to student politics the 'wets' are non-intellectual and the Socialists are mystics. The very simplicity of the distinction between Right and Wrong becomes as easy as Right and Left. The burden of traditional Toryism and its original sin premise can be dropped in favour of a virtue-versus-evil world-view. To give socialism the credibility of a reasonable case to answer is to give the 'sanction of the victim', the worst possible mistake for an individualist to make.

Rand's theory of rights is inextricably linked to her conception of human nature. For her, 'the source of rights is man's nature'.[22] 'Rights are a necessary condition of [Man's] particular mode of survival.'[23]

> Thus for every individual, a right is the moral sanction of a positive of his freedom to act on his own judgment, for his own goals, by his own voluntary, uncoerced choice. As to his neighbours, his rights impose no obligations on them except of a negative kind; to abstain from violating his rights.[24]

Life is not guaranteed. In recognition of this metaphysical fact, Rand holds that rights are freedoms of action and not guarantees of anything. Property rights are not conceived by her to be rights to things, but only the freedom to pursue courses of action with respect to material goods. If certain goods and services are to be guaranteed to individuals – as welfare rights theorists demand – some people, by implication, must be coerced to provide for others. Apart from the fact that what is guaranteed is conditional upon the productivity of some (and hence no guarantee at all), there is in principle no limit to what one could claim must be guaranteed: 'But this view of rights makes a mockery of the notion of a guarantee; for if there is no object to which one may not claim a right, then we could conceivably ask the state to guarantee all things equally, to everyone.'[25] In one fell swoop the Welfare State becomes not merely 'ineffective' – Hayek's ground for opposition – but actually a fraud. The NUS demand for a 'decent grant' can be dismissed as part of a gang of 'looters' fighting over the pickings. To turn a Socialist slogan on its head once again – education is a privilege and not a right.

However, putting these remarks to one side for a moment, Libertarians complain that few reasons are ever given by welfare theorists as to why the inherently coercive apparatus of the state should be the vehicle for providing certain goods to classes. It is not enough to assume blindly – *a priori* – that the state should (let alone could) provide the goods demanded. For Randians the question is: why are acts of force by the state not subject to the levels of moral condemnation we apply to individuals who take such actions? The Welfare State conception of rights is regarded as being explicitly discriminatory: 'That conception of rights demands that the state treat some individuals differently from others, depending on their particular status in society at a particular time (e.g., whether they are rich or poor).'[26]

Libertarians argue that, despite socialist rhetoric, welfare rights do not suppose that people possess rights. Rather, rights are gifts of the state, and therefore this means that like all benefactors the state possesses the power to remove its generosity when it so desires. Because the state is ultimately its own arbiter it has no obligations to respond efficiently to demand. Because in reality no natural, automatic guarantees are given that men will lead successful lives, welfare is identified as being a metaphysical fraud. Welfare theory distorts the true nature of social existence. For Rand the best we can do is to establish conditions which will allow for choices that are essential for the pursuit of life. To establish these social conditions without reference to anyone's particular circumstances is to treat each individual equally.

For her, property rights essentially mean the right to certain courses of action – rather than to particular objects. Property rights are primarily articulated as the right to life; the right of an individual to pursue specific courses of action he thinks best, at any particular time; provided that is he does not interact coercively with others:

> The right to life is the source of all rights – and the right to property is their only implementation. Without property rights, no other rights are possible. Since man has to sustain his life by his own effort, the man who has no right to the product of his effort has no means to sustain his life. The man who produces while others dispose of his product is a slave.[27]

Ayn Rand would no doubt agree, though from an opposing viewpoint, with Mao's statement that 'all political power grows out of the barrel of a gun'.

At the centre of her Objectivist paradigm is the view that because men are physical entities who require material goods to sustain their very existence, the creation, use and disposal of material things must be permitted. Rand holds that as only individuals act, and that therefore collectivities are by definition antithetical constructs, collectivities posses no rights. Thus, as rights specify freedom of action and collectivities do not act, property rights can be possessed only by individuals. Although individuals can form groups and agree to be treated as if they were one, as in the case of a corporation, this does not remove from us the truth that rights ultimately belong to individual human beings. Therefore, property rights demand firstly that individuals must not be kept from seeking material goods, and secondly that they must be free to utilise the goods they have freely acquired.

For Rand, the fact that capitalism involves the pursuit of self-interest is not only correct but morally virtuous. Objectivists argue that
capitalism induces, through the process of individual rational self-
interest, material advancement.

> Whatever one's line of work, a competitive and free market tends to
> push one toward the achievement of the best one is able to produce
> within a given context. Because there are no guarantees that past achieve-
> ments will be not bettered, there are strong incentives to continue to pro-
> duce at the maximum level. Moreover, those who are innovative and
> hard-working are not held to the level of the mediocre and the slothful,
> since there is the full expectation of reaping the rewards of one's efforts.
> In short, capitalism is a system directed toward achievement.[28]

Rand maintained that competition is not the law of the jungle. 'The
motto "dog-eat-dog",' she wrote 'is not applicable to capitalism nor
to dogs.'[29]

> Competition is not a zero-sum game where someone wins and another
> loses, such that there is no overall gain between parties. Competition is
> rather a method of co-ordinating activities in which those who are most
> efficient at utilizing a given resource are in a position to do so. A kind of
> human ecological balance is promoted by the market. An economy of
> resources develops with the result that the appropriate quantity of goods
> of optimal quality are directed into those areas where they are most
> needed or desired.[30]

Countering the Marxist claim that progress under capitalism is
the result of exploiting the surplus labour of workers, Rand contends
that capitalism totally removes sacrifice from human interaction.
The popular belief that capitalism exploits workers is contested. Collectivism, in whatever variety, is a system wherein some are sacri-
ficed for the sake of others. At the root of collectivism's sacrificial
nature is the willingness to operationalise the holistic 'needs of society' view and thereby override individual interests:

> The social theory of ethics substitutes 'society' for God – and through it
> claims that its chief concern is life on Earth, it is not the life of man, not
> the life of an individual, but the life of a disembodied entity ... the col-
> lective. As far as the individual is concerned, his ethical duty is to be the
> selfless, voiceless, rightless slave of any need, claim or demand asserted
> by others.[31]

For Rand, surplus – or profit – is the product of individuals, not a
class phenomenon. In a capitalist society no one is coerced to associate with other individuals if one finds it detrimental to personal
interests. This is not to deny that difficult choices or disagreeable situations cannot be avoided. But capitalism holds the promise that the
products of one's own efforts will not be expropriated without one's

agreement. Marx's claim that under a capitalist class system the proletariat is robbed of the fruits of its labour is rebutted by Rand who
argues that, on the contrary, capitalism is all about the protection of
the fruits of one's labour.

Rand's argument was influential within the FCS, because it discredited the moral basis for a 'Social Revolution' whilst simultaneously offering an ethical case for a 'Capitalist Revolution'. She
argued that no system of *laissez-faire* capitalism has ever existed. And
that, therefore, many of its alleged abuses – depression, poverty, and
war – were instead the result of statism. Having said that, Rand was
no 'anarcho-capitalist'. She always accepted the state's function to
use retaliatory force and believed it should act on behalf of the individual's right to self-defence. Without a set of rules for evidence and
for punishment, there would be no clear way to adjudicate claims
concerning rights violations. Without some specific method of arbi-
tration individuals would not be able to deal with one another in
whatever manner they desired and rights would not be protected at
all. For many Objectivists: 'A further justification for government
lies in the fact that without such protection civilisation would be
impossible, and civilisation is necessary for people to achieve their
proper end as human beings.'[32]

Conservative reaction to Rand's philosophy mirrors an ideological
tension between two prominent post-war factions: traditionalists (the
old-right) and Libertarians (the new-right). Traditionalists who essentially regard Christianity as the moral basis of Western culture regard
Rand's notions of self interest, ethical egoism and *laissez-faire* capitalism as a highway to hell. These 'witch doctors' treat the free market a
natural enemy of their absolute and inflexible beliefs. In America
especially, Rand's criticism of altruism and her praise for capitalism
have been considered as part of the anti-religious message of philosophical materialism. Libertarians, individuals who deny the legitimacy of ethics or consider their enforcement beyond the purview of
the state, are, by and large, ambivalent towards her models of ethical
egoism and *laissez-faire* capitalism. Her commitment to the existence
of objective, moral truths is often thought of as the basis by which
governments can limit liberty and thus pave the way to Fascism.

Going further than Rand, but largely based on her neo-Aris-
totelian natural-law philosophy, the American anarcho-capitalist
Murray Rothbard rejects all forms of statism. Criticising democracy,
he begins by arguing:

> … the identification of the State with society has been redoubled, until it
> is common to hear sentiments expressed which violate virtually every

tenet of reason and common sense: such as 'we are the government'. The useful collective term 'we' has enabled an ideological camouflage to be thrown over the reality of political life ... If 'we are the government,' then anything a government does to an individual is not only just and untyrannical; it is also 'voluntary' on the part of the individual concerned ... Under this reasoning, any Jews murdered by the Nazi government were not murdered; instead, they must have 'committed suicide', since they were the government (which was democratically chosen), and therefore anything the government did to them was voluntary on their part.[33]

In differentiating between politics (the State) and the market Rothbard draws upon the work of the German sociologist Franz Oppenheimer:

[he] pointed out that there are two mutually exclusive ways of acquiring wealth ... one he called the 'economic means'. The other way is simpler in that it does not require productivity; it is the way of seizure of another's goods or services by the use of force and violence. This is the method of one sided confiscation, of theft of the property of others. This is the method which Oppenheimer termed 'the political means' to wealth. It should be clear that the peaceful use of one's reason and energy in production is the 'natural' path for man: the means for his survival and prosperity on earth. It should be equally clear that the coercive, exploitative means is contrary to natural law; it is parasitic, for instead of adding to production, it subtracts from it. The 'political means' siphons production off to a parasitic and destructive individual or group; and this siphoning not only subtracts from the number producing, it also lowers the producer's incentive to produce beyond his own subsistence. In the long run, the robber destroys his own subsistence by dwindling or eliminating the source of his own supply. But not only that; even in the short run, the predator is acting contrary to his own true nature as a man.[34]

When applied by the FCS such ideas led them to denounce politics as a subversive activity alien to a free society. An election would be regarded as merely 'an auction of stolen property' and the Conservative Party's policies rendered almost indistinguishable from those of the Soviet social-engineering practices of the Stalinist era. An electoral majority could no longer be accepted as sufficient to legitimate the implementation of a political programme. The NUS in particular was regarded as so obviously 'illegitimate' that to accept the right of its leadership to represent students was thought to be almost a crime against humanity.

For Rothbard, states and political systems have never been created by 'social contract', they are born out of conquest and force. Yet he argues that to retain power rulers have to gain the support of a majority of subjects in the long run, otherwise they run the risk of being outweighed by the active resistance of the majority. A state's support need not take the form of active enthusiasm: it may well amount to passive resignation as if to an inevitable law of nature. Transposing

Marx's dominant ideology thesis, he argues that: '... the chief task of the [State's] rulers is always to secure the active or resigned acceptance of the majority of the citizens',[35] and one method of obtaining it is through the creation of vested-interest groups:

> ... the king alone cannot rule; he must have a sizable group of followers who enjoy the prerequisites of rule, i.e., the members of the state apparatus, such as the full-time bureaucracy of the established nobility. But this still secures only a minority of earlier supporters ... the majority must be persuaded by ideology that their government is good, wise, and, at least, inevitable, and certainly better than other conceivable alternatives. Promoting this ideology among the people is the vital social task of the 'intellectuals'. For the masses of men do not create their own ideas, or indeed think through these ideas independently; they follow passively the ideas adopted and disseminated by the body of intellectuals. The intellectuals are therefore the 'opinion-moulders' in society. And since it is precisely a moulding of opinion that the state almost desperately needs, the basis for the age-old alliance between the state and the intellectuals becomes clear.[36]

For the FCS the dominant ideology in British higher education was 'statist' and therefore 'Socialist'. Its purpose was to obscure reality or make distorted claims about the 'free world'; the question of intent was considered irrelevant, the 'fact' of bias and indoctrination was obvious in the context of left-dominated campuses. In reaction to this environment, FCS members at Hull University and Humberside College produced an anarcho-capitalist publication, *The New Right Handbook*, which awarded 'Vladimirs' to the most effective socialist propagandist amongst the university's lecturers.[37]

In Rothbard's *For a New Liberty*, an 'anarcho-capitalist manifesto' is presented. It starts with the view that Libertarianism does not emanate from the Left or the Right.[38] Because Libertarians regard conscription as a form of mass slavery and believe in the individual's absolute right to be 'free' from aggression, they stand foursquare with the 'civil liberties' left in supporting: the freedom to speak, publish, assemble and engage in such 'victimless crimes' as pornography, sexual deviation, and prostitution. On the other hand, since Libertarians oppose the violation of property rights and emphatically oppose government interference in the economy, they are inextricably tied to a system of '*laissez-faire* Capitalism' which is popularly thought of as right wing.

Politically, Rothbard is an eclectic, yet coherent and consistent thinker. He argues for nothing less than one global market, devoid of states and formal political institutions. As an anarcho-capitalist he rejects the statist institutions traditionally favoured by Conservatives. For him, state education is nothing more than a 'middle-class hoax':

... if we are to dragoon the entire youth population into vast prisons in the guise of 'education', with teachers and administrators serving as surrogate wardens and guards, why should we not expect vast unhappiness, discontent, alienation, and rebellion on the part of the nation's youth.[39]

He goes on:

Part of the reason for this tyranny ... is misplaced altruism on the part of the educated middle class. The workers, or the 'lower classes', they felt, should have the opportunity to enjoy the schooling the middle classes value so highly. And if the parents or the children of the masses should be so benighted as to balk at this glorious opportunity set before them, well, then a little coercion must be applied – 'for their own good, of course.'[40]

For Rothbard these 'middle-class school worshippers'[41] misunderstand the nature of real education:

Education is a lifelong process of learning, and learning takes place not only in school, but in all areas of life. When the child plays, or listens to parents or friends, or reads a newspaper, or works at a job, he or she is becoming educated. Formal schooling is only a small part of the educational process, and is really only suitable for formal subjects of instruction, particularly in the more advanced and systematic subjects.[42]

Therefore for him:

... the very nature of the [state] school requires the imposition of uniformity and the stamping out of diversity and individuality in education. For it is in the nature of any governmental bureaucracy to live by a set of rules, and to impose those rules in a uniform ... manner. If it did not do so, and the bureaucrats were to decide individual cases ad hoc, he would then be accused, and properly so, of not treating each taxpayer and citizen in an equal and uniform manner. He would be accused of discrimination and of fostering special privilege. Furthermore, it is administratively more convenient for the bureaucrat to establish uniform rules throughout his jurisdiction. In contrast to the private, profit-making business, the government bureaucrat is neither interested in efficiency nor in serving his customers to the best of his ability. Having no need to make profits and sheltered from the possibility of suffering losses, the bureaucrat can and does disregard the desires and demands of his consumer-customers. His major interest is in 'not making waves,' and this he accomplishes by even-handedly applying a uniform set of rules, regardless of how inapplicable they may be in any given case.[43]

As the arguments of Hayek, Nozick, Rand, and Rothbard demonstrate, Libertarians are divided between liberals and anarchists. Liberal-Libertarians like Hayek, Nozick and even Rand may consider the necessity of a 'night watchman state' to protect the market place from disruption (i.e., war, crime or monopoly). They consider justice from a 'Merit' viewpoint. The market is assumed to be capable of distributing goods and services in an equitable and 'just' manner. In contrast, Anarcho-Capitalist Libertarians like Rothbard may ultimately reject 'Rights' as justifying the establishment of authority.[44] They will consider the market as sufficient to the requirements of 'Justice'. Both types of Libertarian ideology could be found within the FCS, although these important differences rarely created much internal discord.

The importance of these authors and ideas is that they provided the FCS with a 'sound' youth consciousness. While Conservative youth had not traditionally based its views on any firm philosophical or ideological grounds, Libertarianism had at its heart a logic that could answer all questions and order the world. The articulation of the pure free market intellectualised student Conservatism in a way that had never been achieved before. As one ex-FCS member has put it:

> Pressing government for sport subsidies has been overtaken. Whereas young Conservatives were traditionally anti-political ideas and politically uninterested, FCS represented the development of a coherent youth consciousness within the party previously never known.[45]

3.3 The Iconography of Libertarian and Anarcho-Capitalist Activism and the Role of Pseudo-Leftist Emulation

During the early 1980s British campuses were uninviting places for Conservative students. With the government's determination to restructure industry along more competitive lines and with rising unemployment, Conservative students found themselves at the sharp end of harsh socialist accusations. As university campuses across the country reacted to 'Thatcherism' and underwent a 'neo-1968 Marcusian revival', many questions were raised that the young right found difficult to answer given their traditional philosophical armoury. What moral justification could they give for such high unemployment? How could Conservatives morally accept the demise of so many British firms? And why did they never appear to care actively about, or campaign on behalf of, the ethnic minorities, the poorly paid, the sick and the infirm?[46]

In an attempt to regain political credibility with other students and attract new supporters many FCS members were attracted to Libertarianism because it not only countered the 'moral' plinth of 'the collectivist mentality', but made them look as dynamic, radical and justified in their beliefs as their ideological opponents. It is important to understand that the 'second wave' of FCS Libertarians were not simply the product of the 'first wave' (that is, purely the consequence of the continuing activities of, for example, the St Andrews Set), but the product of the political environment on campuses and beyond. Because the FCS's Libertarianism, as a form of virulent anti-statism, directly reflected in many ways the left's 'alternative society' model, Conservative students transposed many stylistic elements that were themselves more iconographically attributable to images associated with various forms of orthodox Socialism than to anything previously thought of as Conservative. In using Libertarian economics and stylistically emulating the student left, the FCS quickly earned the reputation of being a hard hitting political force to be reckoned with, characteristics that previous generations of Conservative students had only dreamed of.

As time went on, members of the FCS came to believe that their movement was at the forefront of the 'Thatcherite Revolution', and they defined their battle on two fronts. Firstly, they had a heroic self-image of on-campus political soldiery. They regarded themselves as being in the political front line of vehement anti-Thatcherite hostility and of directly facing the 'massed ranks' of banner-waving, Socialist-slogan-shouting, union-meeting-attending agitators. Secondly, they saw themselves as the intellectual élite of the Conservative Party, individuals who did not simply understand and believe in Thatcherism, but who commanded a paradigm that would extend and 'purify' the revolution. Libertarianism brought to Conservative students a vitality and confidence that they had not experienced before.

For Richard Kelly, in his book *Conservative Party Conferences: The Hidden System*, the FCS's 1986 conference at Scarborough came as quite a surprise:

> ... having attended as an ordinary representative eight years previously ... the contrast between the 1978 and 1986 Conferences was quite shocking. The 1978 Conference had been relatively polite, respectful to the Party hierarchy, faintly 'Heathite' and apparently dominated by the products of independent schools. The mood of the 1986 Conference was much more aggressive and vulgar. Although FCS had already acquired something of a reputation as a stronghold of 'Libertarianism', it was still surprising to witness the zeal with which so many had taken up the cause of 'doctrinaire Conservatism'.[47]

Underlining the similarity between various aspects of the FCS and traditional forms of Socialist student culture, Kelly observed:

> Despite their abhorrence of anything to the 'left' of Margaret Thatcher, it was easy to infer that many representatives were, in fact, of a 'left-wing'

temperament ... the 'sociological' jargon, the stress upon 'principles' before expediency, the vilification of 'traitors', the penchant for doctrine and self-analysis – all these features are normally associated with leftist as opposed to Conservative politics. It was remarkable that the agenda, laden with attacks on the YC's and Tory 'wets', contained not one motion directly critical of the Labour or Alliance parties.

One explanation for this phenomenon might be that whereas, traditionally, those with a taste for 'ideas' and all-purpose theories were drawn to the left, the advent of Conservative 'libertarianism' has begun to draw such people into the unlikely ranks of the Tory Party.[48]

From the Libertarian's point of view the 'Old Etonian Parliamentary Party' were as much an enemy of Capitalism as were Socialists, Fascists and Nazis. The British 'feudal aristocracy' was just another bastion of state-protected privilege. Instead of operating in the competitive market, they spent their time preoccupied with such 'antihistorical' phenomena as the monarchy, the House of Lords, the civil service and the lobbying of government for ever larger subsidies on their Covent Garden opera seats. The view was commonly held that the British middle classes were increasingly oppressive, coercive and immoral, because they had developed a vast vested interest in statism. Teachers, health workers, social workers and local government 'middle-class trendies' were all perceived as the bureaucratic enemies of liberty and freedom.

Libertarianism not only gave the FCS an intellectual air, but it enabled them stylistically to parody the left and play them at their own 'sociologised game'. This in turn not only served the function of boosting the morale and attractiveness of the FCS, but would directly offend and 'wind up' the left. At times the FCS were attempting to debase traditional student politics. Observing the 1986 FCS Conference, Kelly noted: 'Many representatives plainly enjoyed seeing themselves as "bold", "controversial", "irreverent" and so on – the sort of "qualities" which would have brought great praise from anti-Conservative observers twenty years previously.'[49]

In contrast with the smartly dressed hacks of earlier Conservative student generations, Libertarian activists were distinctly studentish. Very little of mid-1980s striped-shirt yuppy culture, so often popularly associated with Thatcherism, wore off on these activists. Their fashion was a distinctly casual affair. Individuals, and most notably the organisation's national and regional officers, refused to wear the traditional garb of Conservatism. Instead they wore T-shirts, tracksuit bottoms and shabby trainers.

One influential Libertarian student, having identified the development of an abhorrence for 'boring' clothes within Conservative circles, set up a firm called 'Popular Propaganda' to actively promote a distinctive, casual, new style of dress. Paul Staines, a streaked-haired FCS activist from Humberside College, was the quintessential expression of Libertarian youth culture. A dynamic and clever entre-preneur, Staines successfully worked on fusing the ideology of anar-cho-capitalism to the activist style of the traditional student left. Under such headings as 'Fight for the Right', 'Freedom Fighters', 'voluntarily exchange money for goods' and 'Thatcherite hegemony for unity against corporatism', Staines' catalogue advertised items that carried a variety of Libertarian messages. His T-shirt slogans included: 'Privatise Me!'; 'World Wide Capitalism Now'; 'Free Enter-prise, Free Markets, Free People'; 'Nicaragua Must be Free, FDN, Reagan'; 'Victory to Unita'; 'World Peace Through World Trade'.[50]

Challenging notions of socialist internationalism, Staines was a master at associating the ideas of free trade, peace, international free migration and global prosperity. For the FCS membership exposed to, and eager to buy, his goods, Libertarianism was not just right, moral and hence worthy, it had history on its side. The view was internalised throughout the movement that as technology, travel and western corporations globalised, all forms of statism were nothing more than 'anti-historic' and doomed to failure. Culturally, Libertar-ians in the FCS idealised films that depicted a future built upon the commercialisation, rationalisation and instrumentalisation of day-to-day life. The anti-collectivist film *Brazil* was an instant cult success.[51]

The imagery of late-twentieth-century capitalism and its imagined future burned brightly into the day-to-day lives of the FCS's mem-bers. They not only revelled in cultural diversity, but actually sought it on ideological grounds. In contrast with the more xenophobic aspects of traditional Conservatism, foreign restaurants, foreign music and foreigners were not just tolerated but actively supported and held in high esteem. Surely they were early social signposts pointing to a free-trade future where international capitalism would transcend the isolated nation state.

A number of FCS members made a great deal out of socialising in the worst cafés they could find. On one occasion a self-confessed 'anarcho-capitalist' vice-president of a leading London Polytechnic Conservative Association ushered me with haste into 'a great new café' he had found. Not only was the place filthy and the roof actu-ally caving in, but on receiving an order for a prawn cocktail, the proprietor walked into the middle of the restaurant, stuck his bare hands into a fridge freezer, grabbed some prawns, and plunged them directly under a hot water tap so as to effect instant defrosting before immediately stuffing them into a dish ready for consumption there and then. Watching this act of theatrical gastronomy the vice-president beamed and commented: 'It's marvellous – Capitalism!'[52]

Another activist, Brian Micklethwait, Editorial Director of the Libertarian Alliance, asked about his love for some of London's more shoddy cafes, he explained that because these institutions tend to be 'vulgar, tasteless and unhygienic' their owners 'are the enemies of our enemies, and as such are our friends'. Micklethwait argued that they represent 'evidence of free will to do wildly unsavoury things' and as such are fun to observe: 'they break with the monotony of state regulated day-to-day routine'. As the left have become progressively more middle class and respectable, so they have 'turned their backs on the seedy, the unsafe and risky'.[53]

Life in the FCS was rich in pseudo-leftist symbolism and 'street credibility'. Observing this element of the FCS's culture, Kelly asserted, in his analysis of their 1986 conference:

> During the election of 'ordinary' committee members, a rugged Scot called Mark Dingwall seemed to epitomise that element of FCS which Central Office was anxious to suppress. After spelling out his impeccable 'working-class' credentials, and announcing that he had come into politics via a Protestant Orange Lodge in Glasgow, he spoke of his admiration for Derek Hatton and Leninist discipline. 'If you vote for me you can be sure your ideals will be properly represented.' I say 'vote the slate, walk the line.'[54]

Commenting on the conference's foreign policy debate Kelly describes a scene difficult to imagine in Conservative Party circles:

> The main thrust of it attacked 'so-called Liberation movements' (singling out the IRA, PLO and ANC for special opprobrium) and extolled 'anti-totalitarian freedom-fighting movements' like Unita in Angola, the Nicaraguan Contras and the Afghan Mujahidin. The posters bedecking the conference hall suggested a lot of interest in these distant military groups, especially the Contras, which seemed to be a cause close to the hearts of many FCS members. The debate provided an opportunity for David Hoile, a retiring vice-chairman and the driving force behind the FCS Foreign Affairs Group, to enunciate the federations's 'global strategy' ... He argued that FCS should be the catalyst of a new 'international anti-communist brigade' and criticised the Foreign Secretary for 'appeasing Marxist terrorists' (a reference to the campaign for the release of Nelson Mandela). In addition to the 300 word 'main motion', the conference also debated six equally long amendments relating to South Africa, the African National Congress, Angola, Nicaragua and President Reagan's Strategic Defence Initiative ... Subjects tended to overlap and speakers often strayed back into previous amendments. After three hours of deliberately provocative comment on 'foreign policy', representatives even began to lose their ability to shock. The audience seemed unsurprised

when one speaker claimed to have recently served with the 'Lebanese Christian Militia' and there was only a ripple of applause when another described his 'smuggling expeditions to the Soviet Union' ... [55]

During the 1980s members of the FCS established close links with a large number of anti-communist free-market groups at home and abroad. From the anti-CND organisation, the Coalition for Peace Through Security, to Washington's National Centre for Public Policy Research, these activists developed an impressive network. Often operating 'behind enemy lines' in Latin America, Africa, or the Eastern Bloc, FCS Libertarians concentrated on disseminating free market literature and ideas. Hayek, Rand, Nozick and Rothbard were all flown in to countries like Poland, South Africa and the Soviet Union on what were popularly called 'Airborne FCS operations'. These sorties by 'FCS Special Forces'[57] not only served the purpose of taking the 'battle of ideas to the heart of the enemy' (the world's most statist regimes), but served as a type of 'regimental initiation'.

A selection of the artwork used by the FCS on their many varied publications not only aesthetically underlines the group's fundamentalist 'pseudo-leftist style', but also demonstrates a deep affiliation with traditional anti-communist symbols derived from post-war American culture. FCS iconography represented a radical divergence from the Conservative Party's 'normal' publicity in terms of both style and argument.

Figure 3.1 Tory Militant, Pravda, Capitalist Worker

At campus level the FCS set out to carry on guerrilla warfare. The imagery of an FCS branch was deliberately designed to offend the student left and break its hegemony in student affairs by provoking riots, bans, public denunciations and general disruption. Supported by a 'historic destiny' vision of the freedom fighter combating what President Reagan was then calling 'The Evil Empire' and perceiving themselves in the manner of Rand's heroic characters, these 'revolutionary cadres' saw themselves as going to war for 'Life, Liberty and Property'.

As a first step it was inevitable, in order to shock the dominant left, that the heroes and imagery of socialism should be either adopted, parodied, ridiculed or destroyed. The adoption of titles more often associated with 'leftist' groups, '*Tory Militant*', '*Capitalist*

Worker' and '*Pravda*' (figure 3.1) were both typical and widespread. The replacement of Karl Marx and Lenin by Hayek and Tebbit (see *Pravda*) were intended as a tribute to 'our leaders' and evidence that the new Conservatives also had historic figures to emulate.

Figure 3.2 The Feudal Times and Reactionary Herald

Other titles were designed to offend wet enemies within. '*Libertarian Student*', '*Armageddon*', '*The Capitalist*' and even '*Capital*' (a play on London's status as well as Marx's book) all took the form of overt expressions of Libertarianism and were clearly designed to attract condemnation from party officials. This trend was most clearly exemplified by Harry Phibbs' dummy title, '*The Feudal Times and Reactionary Herald*' (figure 3.2), which was the immediate precursor to the ill-fated New Agenda magazine.

The imagery of FCS magazines was often a hybrid of Stalinist propaganda and American pop culture. Examples abound of 'Soldier Of Fortune' style graphics, notably 'Kill a Commie for Mommy', 'Better Dead than Red' (considering CND's membership at the time) and 'Death Before Dishonour' (the motto of the US Marine Corps). As a result of the coincidental appearance of several gung-ho movies, the character Rambo was frequently used. Tebbit or a 'sound' FCS 'comrade' would find his/her head superimposed over that of a Rambo look-alike toting a massive anti-tank weapon (figure 3.3).

The 'elimination' of the FCS's enemies as part of the legitimate armed struggle would involve targeting people in direct proportion to their adulation by socialists. 'Hang Mandela' stickers were released (parodying the song 'Free Mandela') that resembled material issued by the anti-apartheid movement.

Leicester FCS, the self-styled 'Leicester Loonies', held a party to celebrate the second anniversary of the liberation of Grenada by US forces, a great military adventure not least because it caused the 'Communist bureaucrats in the London Foreign Office' grave embarrassment. The Contras in Nicaragua could have been supported for no better reason than that they were killing Sandinistas, the darlings of the British leftist intelligentsia (figure 3.4).

Overall, the 'Libertarian Struggle' was probably best articulated

TEBBO

NO PARTY, NO LABOUR LEADER
CAN STOP HIM NOW.
APPEARING AT A LABOUR HELD SEAT NEAR YOU

Figure 3.3 Tebbo

LEICESTER F.C.S.

GRENADA LIBERATION DAY CELEBRATION

VENUE : 'BELLA MIA'
NEW BOND ST.
LEICESTER   25th October

8 FOR 8·30

DISCO
BAR 'TIL 1·45
FOOD

TWO
YEARS
OF
FREEDOM
!

£ 4·00
DRESS : COMBAT GEAR

Figure 3.4 Grenada Liberation Day Celebration

by David Hoile's 'Conservative Students Foreign Affairs Group' (figure 3.5).

The emotional appeal to free the Third World from the imperialist oppression of the East caused as much criticism within the Conservative Party as horror among the student left.

In the use of pseudo-Socialist artwork for the 'Savimbi' and 'Unita' campaign, one immediately recognises the striking similarity with the 'Castro'/'Che Guevara' image so popular in the late 1960s (figure 3.6).

Leftist emulation was so effective that instances could be found of Socialist students wearing 'Nicaragua must be free' stickers in the belief that they were supporting their own side. The stickers in question even carried the stars and stripes. Obviously, some on the left believed that Conservatives could not possibly be interested in promoting a particular cause in such a faraway Central American country.

To the Conservative student whose digs might be decked with such posters as: 'The forces of Socialism had planned for everything. Except for 14,000 Freedom Fighters called FCS', the world could be broken down into 'sound' and 'unsound'.

The knowledge of one's place in the face of the 'Socialist onslaught' in the universities and colleges at the time of the Falklands, the Brighton bombing, the CND revival and the Miners' Strike was a comforting one if your ideology presents you with the argument and conviction that your personal views as a Conservative are still right. It is noticeable that during the early 1980s many in the YCs kowtowed to the socialist consensus. For a Libertarian in FCS to support a national campaign on youth homelessness, drug abuse and unemployment was not only a total contradiction between beliefs and action but also a shameful surrender to the socialist

MNR RENAMO
MOZAMBIQUE
THE STRUGGLE CONTINUES
CONSERVATIVE STUDENTS FOREIGN AFFAIRS GROUP

Figure 3.5
Mozambique: The Struggle Continues

Savimbi

Unita

Figure 3.6 Savimbi, UNITA

agenda. The FCS would not even debate some of the issues campaigned on by the YCs during this period. After all, those FCS comrades who had read Ayn Rand's *The Fountainhead* would have taken to heart Howard Roark's courtroom speech:

Throughout the centuries there were men who took first steps down new roads armed with nothing but their own vision. Their goals differed, but they all had this in common; that the step was first, the road new, the vision unborrowed, and the response they received – hatred... . Every great new thought was opposed. Every great new invention was denounced... . But the men of unborrowed vision went ahead. They fought, they suffered and they paid. But they won.[57]

For FCS members the issue of NUS membership was one of the most bitter areas in which they could express their ideology. Isadora Duncan, the early sympathiser and promoter of the Bolshevik revolution, was 'usurped' for the anti-NUS campaign at a time when the hard left was glorifying 1930s Soviet propagandist art (figure 3.7).

Not only is the slogan an obvious parody of the *Communist Party Manifesto* by Marx and Engels,[58] but the poster could be an exhortation to work harder for the Revolution from the early Stalinist period.

As the FCS's battle progressed, their imagery became associated with the left's 'armed struggle' and in some cases reflected the urban guerrilla outlook. The development along with the simultaneous shift in style towards American comic strip also led to the emulation of cartoon characters almost invariably American. As an illustration the presentation of a Libertarian line under the heading 'Superheroes' was typical. Other examples included Conan style gladiators, Batman-style scenes with speech bubbles referring to internal FCS struggles and comic strip violence depicting the fate that awaited the 'enemies of freedom'.

Much of the 'best' FCS material was linked with the anti-NUS campaign. Its aim was to create a feeling of moral superiority for the FCS whilst simultaneously insulting the entire union hierarchy, and often in fairly crude terms. 'Nuke NUS', for example, clearly set out to anger those in power (figure 3.8).

Freedom lovers of the world unite! Throw off the NUS chains! Liberate Your Union!

Figure 3.7 Freedom Lovers of the World Unite!

Violent symbols such as the sinking of the Belgrano (figure 3.9) were often used for the sole purpose of creating a riot by NUS and thereby justifying its abolition.

On a more positive note, whilst still causing offence to wets and external opponents, the promotion of a vanguard Thatcherite view was adopted by the FCS. To a Libertarian any suggestion that the slogan 'Capitalism the Democratic Economy' was controversial, let alone offensive, would be quite absurd. However, given the normal dominance of posters produced by the Socialist Workers Party on campuses, this almost naïve slogan could cause a reaction by the left completely disproportionate to the intended effect.

Figure 3.8 Nuke NUS

Figure 3.9 We Sunk the Belgrano and We'll Sink NUS

In a similar vein, *Blue Touchpaper* – a *New Agenda* imitation – could offend the left, as well as the Conservative Party's officials, almost without trying. A serious discussion of the merits of Bob Geldof's Band Aid, and the presumed futility of assisting a Marxist regime, was tied to the sanctions issue in South Africa and resulted in the 'Socialism Kills – Free Markets Feed' campaign (figure 3.10).

To the left it was deeply offensive, to CCO it was, at best, tasteless. Other campaigns where the FCS would take a 'safe' issue like privatisation, it would be applied to British Rail and the National Coal Board precisely when these industries were in the grips of strikes (figure 3.11).

The NUS conference led to disruption and widespread rule breaking. The ban on 'sexism' provoked the FCS riposte 'Support the Cuts!' – not of public expenditure but of a woman's bra straps (figure 3.12).

The extremism of the FCS, on drugs deregulation and the age of consent, eventually led to self-mockery, exemplified by the child sex cartoon taken from the SFCS magazine *Armageddon* (figure 3.13).

Figure 3.10 Blue Touchpaper Free Markets Feed

Figure 3.11 *This is the Age of Privatisation, Privatise the Pits*

Figure 3.12 *Support the Cuts*

The hardening of FCS ideology can be traced through the movement's iconographic development. The 1984 Durham University *Defender* with its 'Crimes of the Gang of Four: Creation of the Permissive Society', through to the 1986 *Armageddon* previously mentioned, clearly shows the progression of Libertarian ideas from moral authoritarianism and economic liberty towards total permissiveness, via a desire to shock 'wets' and 'other socialists'.

What may have started as imitation because of a lack of 'Conservative' icons, gradually built into a gallery of 'heroes' and 'villains' with the development of an impressive array of styles and themes. It is almost certain that some policy orientations followed, not merely from the reading of sound literature, but from the need to follow up the destruction of a Socialist slogan with one promoting a positive cause. The 'Hang Mandela' slogan tacked on to a 'Free Mandela' poster was the logical precursor for 'Viva Savimbi'. If Unita had not existed, the FCS would have perhaps invented it.

Figure 3.13 *Child Sex Cartoon*

Notes and References

1. There does not appear to be any particular – easily accessible – reason why the student Libertarians emerged first at St Andrews University. For more on the subject see: *Scotsman*, 9 September 83, p. 7; *Glasgow Herald*, 10 June 89, p. 10; *Glasgow Herald*, 7 August 91. Although St Andrews University was the main staging post for the FCS's Libertarian 'first wave' as it appeared in the 1970s, a number of members at the London School of Economics held similar views. John Blundell, the current General Director of the Institute of Economic Affairs was one such individual who espoused radical free market ideas as a student.
2. See: *Scotsman*, 13 August 90; *Scotsman*, 8 September 90; *Guardian*, 8 September 90; *Glasgow Herald*, 22 October 90. Also see: *Daily Record*, 5 October 90.
3. *Observer*, 7 April 85.

4. See: Pirie, M., (1992) *Blueprint for a Revolution*, London, ASI (Research) Ltd.
5. Pirie, M., 'The Cross of St Andrews' in *Freedom First: The Journal of the Society for Individual Freedom*, No. 76, Summer 1989, p. 16.
6. Ibid.
7. Pirie, M., 'The Cross'.
8. Ibid.
9. This point has also been observed by Toby Young in the *Observer*, 7 April 85.
10. Hayek, F. A., (1944) *The Road to Serfdom*, London, Routledge and Kegan Paul.
11. See: Graham, D. and Clarke, P., (1986) *The New Enlightenment*, London, Macmillan in association with Channel 4, p. 7. Regarding the 'Austrian School of Economics' see: Barry, N. P., (1979) *Hayek's Social and Economic Philosophy*, London, Macmillan. Butler, E., (1983) *Hayek: His Contribution to the Political and Economic Thought of our Time*, Hounslow, Temple Smith. Dolan, E. G., (ed.) (1976) *The Foundations of Modern Austrian Economics*, Kansas City, Sheed & Ward. Friedman, M., (1962) *Capitalism and Freedom*, Chicago, The University Press. Friedman, M., and Friedman, R., (1980) *Free to Choose*, Harmondsworth, Penguin Books. Friedman, M. and Friedman, R., (1985) *The Tyranny of the Status Quo*, Harmondsworth, Penguin Books. Grassl, W. and Smith, B., (eds) (1986) *Austrian Economics*, London, Croom Helm. Hayek, F. A., (1980) *Individualism and Economic Order*, Chicago, University of Chicago Press, Midway reprint. Hayek, F. A., (1984) *Money, Capital and Fluctuations*, edited by R. McCloughry, London, Routledge. Kirzner, I., (1986) *Subjectivism, Intelligibility and Economic Understanding*, London, Macmillan. Lachmann, L. M., (1977) *Capital, Expectations and Market Process*, Kansas City, Sheed, Andrews & McMeel. Mises, L. von (1966) *Human Action*, 3rd revised edn, Chicago, Contemporary Books. Mises, L. von (1978) *Ultimate Foundations of Economic Science*, Kansas City, Sheed, Andrews & McMeel. Mises, L. von (1981) *Socialism*, Indianapolis, Liberty Fund. Rothbard, M. N., (ed.) (1987) *The Review of Austrian Economics*, Vol. 1, Lexington, Mass, D. C. Heath. Spadaro, L. M., (ed.) (1978) *New Directions in Austrian Economics*, Kansas City, Sheed, Andrews & McMeel.
12. Hayek, F. A., (1976) *Law, Legislation and Liberty*, Vol. 2., *The Mirage of Social Justice*, London, Routledge and Kegan Paul, pp. 70-1.
13. Nozick, R., (1974) *Anarchy, State and Utopia*, Oxford, Basil Blackwell.
14. Rand, A., (1967) 'What is Capitalism' in *Capitalism the Unknown Ideal*, New York, New American Library, p. 20. See also: Branden, N. and Branden, B., (1964) *Who Is Ayn Rand?*, New York, Paperback Library. Branden, B., (1986) *The Passion of Ayn Rand*, London, W. H. Allen & Co. Branden, N., (1985) *Judgement Day: My Years with Ayn Rand*, New York, Houghton Mifflin. Mevrill, R. E., (1991) *The Ideas of Ayn Rand*, Lasalle, Illinois, Open Court.
15. Den Uyl, D. and Rasmussen, D. B., (eds) (1986) *The Philosophic Thought of Ayn Rand*, Illinois, Illinois University Press, p. 166.
16. Rand, A., *Capitalism the Unknown Ideal*, p. 19.
17. Ibid.
18. Rand, A., (1961) *For the New Intellectual*, New York, Signet Books, p. 14.
19. Ibid.
20. Ibid.
21. Ibid., p. 15.
22. Rand, A., *Capitalism the Unknown Ideal*, p. 322.
23. Ibid.
24. Ibid.
25. Den Uyl, D and Rasmussen, D. B., *The Philosophical Thought*, p. 169.
26. Ibid.
27. Rand, A., *Capitalism the Unknown Ideal*, p. 20. See also: Den Uyl, D. and Rasmussen, D. B., (eds) *The Philosophic Thought*, p. 174.
28. See: Rand, A., *Capitalism the Unknown Ideal*, p. 20. See also: Den Uyl, D. and Rasmussen, D. B. (eds) *The Philosophical Thought*, p. 174.
29. Rand, A., (1964) *The Virtue of Selfishness*, New York, New American Library, p. 34.

30. Den Uyl, D. and Rasmussen, D. B., (eds) *The Philosophical Thought*, pp. 174-175.
31. Rand, A., *The Virtue of Selfishness*, p. 34.
32. Den Uyl, D. and Rasmussen, D. B., (eds) *The Philosophical Thought*, p. 178.
33. Rothbard, M. N., 'The Anatomy of The State' in *Rampart Journal of Individualist Thought*, Vol. 1, No. 2, Summer, 1965.
34. Ibid. See also: Oppenheimer, F., (1926) *The State*, New York, Vanguard Press, pp. 24-7.
35. Ibid.
36. Ibid.
37. *The Right Handbook*, (1986) Hull University and Humberside College FCS, p. 30. This book produced by Paul Staines was a masterful example of FCS anarcho-capitalist iconography. The back cover reads: 'NEITHER SOCIALISM OR CONSERVATISM BUT LIBERTY – DEATH TO THE REVISIONIST ENEMIES OF THE GLORIOUS THATCHERITE REVOLUTION – DESTROY THE NUS IMPERIALISTS – RESIST THE HEATHITE LACKEYS OF COLLECTIVISM – ONLY THROUGH CONSTANT VIGILANCE AND LOYALTY TO THE PARTY CAN WE ACHIEVE THE HAYEKIAN IDEAL – YOUTH OF THE WORLD THROW OFF YOUR CHAINS AND RISE UP AGAINST YOUR NUS OVERLORDS – THE BOURGEOIS SOCIALIST YOKE MUST BE UNSHACKLED – THROUGH STUDY AND ADHERENCE TO HAYEKIAN-THATCHERISM THE PARTY WILL BE AT THE FOREFRONT OF THE INTELLECTUAL VANGUARD – REJECT WET EMPIRICISM – A THOUSAND DEFEATS TO THE ENEMIES OF THE MUJAHIDIN – BEWARE OF WET REVISIONISTS – SPONTANEOUS ORDER DEMANDS THE DESTRUCTION OF THE STATE – FREE ENTERPRISE – FREE MARKETS – FREE PEOPLE – ONLY THROUGH EXERCISING LENINIST DISCIPLINE CAN THE REVOLUTIONARY CADRES MAINTAIN THEIR VANGUARD ROLE – SOLIDARITY WITH THE LIBERATION OF ANGOLA AND MOZAMBIQUE – VICTORY TO SAVIMBI – TAXATION IS THEFT – SOCIALISM IS THE RED BRICK ROAD TO SERFDOM – DEFEAT TO THE ANTI-ZIONIST RACISTS – FREE THE PROLETARIAT FROM STATE SLAVERY WE MUST WORK FOR THE FINAL VICTORY OF CAPITALISM – TELL'EM TEBBIT – LIBERATE HAVANA, MOSCOW, TRIPOLI, MANAGUA AND KABUL – SING SOUND SLOGANS ... '. On page 7 of this anarchic publication appears a letter from Prime Minister Margaret Thatcher. She wrote: 'I send you every good wish in all you are doing to promote the Conservative cause in Hull.' Under her remarks, Hull FCS add an advertisement. It read: 'JOIN THE RESISTANCE – THE FEDERATION OF CONSERVATIVE STUDENTS. FCS CADRES ARE THE NUCLEUS OF THE LIBERTARIAN MOVEMENT – ONLY FCS FIGHTS FOR FREEDOM – NO OTHER STUDENT MOVEMENT HAS AT ITS CORE A PHILOSOPHY OF INDIVIDUAL LIBERTY – NO OTHER MOVEMENT IS AS DYNAMICALLY VIBRANT – ACCEPT NO OTHERS – THE ALTERNATIVE IS SERFDOM ... WARNING DO NOT JOIN IF YOU ARE RACIST, MONARCHIST OR NATIONALIST – FASCISTS ARE ADVISED TO JOIN THE LABOUR PARTY – ANARCHISTS ARE WELCOME TO THE PARTY.'
38. Rothbard, M. N., (1973) *For a New Liberty*, New York, The Macmillan Publishing Co.
39. Ibid., p. 132.
40. Ibid., pp. 132-3.
41. Ibid., p. 133.
42. Ibid.
43. Ibid., pp. 140-1.
44. See: Benson, B. L., (1990) *The Enterprise of Law: Justice Without the State*, San Francisco, Pacific Research Institute for Public Policy.

45. Quote from a recorded interview with an ex-FCS member in South-East Area who wished to remain anonymous.

46. For an informative analysis on political polarisation at this time see: Therbon, G., 'West On The Dole', in *Marxism Today*, June 1985.

47. Kelly, N. R., (1989) *Conservative Party Conferences: The Hidden System*, Manchester, Manchester University Press, pp. 114-15.

48. Ibid., p. 115.

49. Ibid., p. 105.

50. Popular Propaganda catalogue produced by Paul Staines and distributed to Conservative students, 1986. For more on Staines see: Staines, P., (1991) *Acid House Parties Against The Lifestyle Police and The Safety Nazis*, Political Notes No. 55, London, Libertarian Alliance.

51. *Brazil:* Terry Gilliam's portrayal of statism in the twentieth century was released in 1985.

52. An ex-FCS London region member who wishes to remain anonymous, during a private meeting with the author.

53. Brian Micklethwait, editorial director of the Libertarian Alliance during a telephone interview with the author. Micklethwait argues that the free market is the best regulator of goods and services. That by encouraging competition and innovation markets automatically raise standards and improve service quality: 'those who want regulations can get them on the market'. For more information see: Micklethwait, B., (1993) *How and How Not to Achieve Good Taste in Advertising: Free Market Regulation is Better than Government Regulation*, Political Notes No. 74, London, Libertarian Alliance.

54. Kelly, R., *Conservative Party Conferences*, p. 106.

55. Ibid., p. 107.

56. 'FCS Special Forces' was the term used by 'sound' FCS members when any anti-communist activity was actively engaged in. It was a term particularly used by the FCS vice-chairman David Hoile. He also coined the phrase 'Airborne FCS' used to describe members attending anti-left demonstrations, meetings and conferences in the UK and beyond. Brian Micklethwait, editorial director of the Libertarian Alliance, and a number of other LA subscribers and activists, visited Eastern Europe to advise on computers, desktop publishing and political campaigning. Many of these operations were organised by Brian Crozier. See: Crozier, B., (1993) *Free Agent: The Unseen War 1941-1991*, London, Harper Collins.

57. Rand, A., (1943) *The Fountainhead*, New York, The Bobbs-Merrill Company, pp. 736-7.

58. See Marx, K., and Engels, F., (1848) *Manifest der Kommunistischen Partei*. Authorised English translation by: Samuel Moore, with introduction and notes by Engels (1888).

Chapter IV

THE THIRD GENERATION
The Continued Libertarianisation of
Conservative Youth Structures

....

Although the FCS was disbanded by the Conservative Party in the autumn of 1986, the Libertarians did not fade away. Within a short period of time both the party's new student group, the 'Conservative Collegiate Forum' and the YCs began to adopt a philosophical world-view based upon Libertarian and anarcho-capitalist ideas. This chapter begins by outlining the nature of these developments and goes on to present a comparative organisational analysis.

4.1 The Libertarian Permeation of the Conservative Collegiate Forum

In November 1986[1] the Conservative Party announced that the affairs of Conservative students were to be managed in future by a new group called the 'Conservative Collegiate Forum' (CCF). At the time CCO expressed the coded wish that this group would be 'more representative of Conservative student opinion' and clearly hoped it would go a long way towards removing the problem of Libertarianism. While the mechanics of the CCF took around a year to finalise, it was clear from the outset that its members were not going to have the kind of autonomy and freedom the FCS had enjoyed. There were to be no annual elections. Instead, officers at national and regional levels were to be appointed directly by senior Party officials.

Notes for this section begin on page 96.

However, as soon as it became apparent that the party was going to reorganise Conservative student affairs in an attempt to curb Libertarian influence, many in the FCS began to adopt new tactics. One of their first objectives was to take over the National Association of Conservative Graduates (NACG).[2] This relatively minor organisation catering for Conservatives who have completed their degrees was quickly seized upon and used as a staging post from which to influence not only the new CCF, but also the YCs. Another group of Libertarians set up a totally new organisation outside the party's formal structure and called it 'Conservative Students' (CS). Organised from London, this group provided a number of ex-FCS activists with a firm base from which to target the party's youth wings.[3]

Although the Libertarians might be charged with undertaking a well-thought-out, highly disciplined, entryist strategy, in reality there was no co-ordinating committee, no central command structure directing events. Instead, the activists involved simply formed part of a spontaneous, diffuse and largely unco-ordinated network of highly motivated ideologues. Recounting his experiences in late 1986 one ex-FCS activist tells a typical story: 'I could see the end of FCS coming. So I joined the local Young Conservative branch instead. I made sure we had a Libertarian chairman there within six months.'[4] The Libertarians did not need co-ordinating. Their strength lay in their motivation to act independently on initiative. After all, this mode of action was at the very heart of their individualist philosophy.

For many of the older Libertarians the closure of the FCS made little difference, nearing graduation their minds were turning to the world beyond student politics anyway. For those considering a political career, the world of pressure group politics seemed a wise and natural choice. Since the late 1970s the Conservative Party has been flanked by a growing number of free-market policy institutes where ex-FCS activists could feel at home. Influential organisations like the Adam Smith Institute, the Institute of Economic Affairs, and the Libertarian Alliance all attracted ex-members of the FCS's second wave. These groups offered varying degrees of indirect logistical support for those who wanted to remain involved in the battle of ideas within the NACG, CCF and YCs. Whereas many from the FCS's first generation had now entered parliament, or reached senior positions in pressure groups, the second generation provided cheap labour and fresh intellectual blood.

Because the Conservative Party believed that Libertarianism was the result of organised militancy on the part of a number of key individuals it decided to hand-pick a new generation of CCF national and regional officers. Confident that they had not held senior posi-

tions within the FCS, the party believed that the problem of extremism would go away. However, within two years the organisation was
not only back in Libertarian hands, but was as ideologically pure as
the FCS, if not more so. Within three months, commentators began
to notice that everything was not going to CCO's plan. Under the
heading 'Long march for the loony right' Nick Palmer wrote in the
Communist Party of Great Britain's newspaper, *7 Days Perspective*:

> Despite the closure of the FCS which, for the time being, removed from
> the Libertarians' grasp the only official part of the Conservative Party
> they ever controlled, the 'Radical Thatcherites' are here to stay. With
> some justice they claim to have won the ideological battle within the party
> and now they have a firm group of MP supporters, some of whom have
> come up through the FCS. There can be little doubt that their ideas will
> influence, and perhaps dominate, the post-Thatcher Conservative Party.[5]

By July 1987 articles began to appear which confirmed CCO's
worst fears. Under the headline 'Young Tories fund Contra terrorists',
Tony Clark of the *Morning Star* reported:

> CONTRA terror squads operating inside Nicaragua are being sponsored
> by young Conservatives in Britain.
>   It is being supported by British Young Conservatives and Conserva-
> tive Students.
>   The shock revelations came from right-wing young Tory Marc Gordon
> who has just returned from an eight-day armed stay with Contra terrorists
> operating in Honduras and Nicaragua.
>   Tory MP's and right business people are reported to have funded Mr
> Gordon's trip.
>   [...] The 21-year-old Birmingham University graduate claims to be
> vice-chair of West Midlands Conservative Students and a past county
> chair of Cornwall Young Conservatives.
>   He is reported to have access to the House of Commons and will
> debrief Tory MP's about his mission.
>   Embarrassed Tory Party Office spokes-persons yesterday desperately
> tried to distance themselves from Mr. Gordon's activities, claiming that
> he has no direct link with the Party.
>   The Conservative Students Foreign Affairs group, of whom Mr Gor-
> don claims to be the vice-chair, is not an official Party organisation.
>   But he clearly has the sympathy of right-wing elements whose active
> Contra support directly conflicts with Foreign Office policy.[6]

Although the FCS had been closed in an attempt to halt the rise
of Libertarianism, by 1988 the definition of what it was to be 'middle-of-the-road' had itself been substantially re-defined and pulled to
the free market right. The 1988 *London Conservative Collegiate Forum
Handbook* demonstrated just how acceptable Libertarian ideas had
become. In an article, entitled 'Fighting for our Freedom', student
activist Ian Martin wrote:

Many people are expressing concern about some of the more restrictive and authoritarian tendencies in Government policy. They observe that the principles of freedom and responsibility in the economic spheres of Government policy do not extend to other spheres. The setting up of the new television watchdog, the rushed restrictions on firearms, the Home Secretary prepared to consider curtailing the right to silence of suspects, the proposals to raise drink prices to stop the few abusing alcohol, and so the list goes on of restrictions rather than de-regulation. If people can be trusted with economic freedom, why not with social freedom and responsibility?[7]

It was not long before CCO had to acknowledge the CCF's demand for Libertarian ideas and radical iconography. The officially sanctioned poster '1917–1979 – Revolutions – The Difference is Capitalism' (figure 4.1) demonstrated just how far the free market right had come. This was a poster FCS members would have been proud to display.

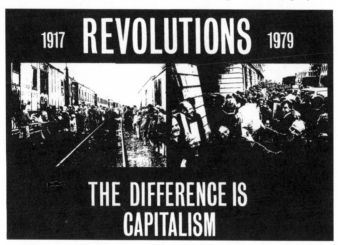

Figure 4.1 1917-1979 Revolutions: The Difference is Capitalism

The *1989 Scottish Conservative Colegiate Forum Conference Magazine* included two Libertarian articles that resembled the tone of FCS publications. In the first, entitled 'Who's Right', Martin Burns wrote:

In deciding the political wing on to which a government should be placed, greater weight must be given to the effect rather than the method of government. The aim of this article is to redefine the political spectrum in a manner to which everyone can relate.[8]

For Burns the 'wing on to which a government should be placed' was measured according to the degree of statism it incorporates. Hence the political spectrum 'left to right' was reproduced as shown in figure 4.2.[9] The article presented a brief description of each of these political schools. Under the heading 'Anarchal Capitalism' it stated:

'ANARCHAL CAPITALISM prevails when the state does not exist at all. Protection is provided by private security firms employed by individuals and companies.'[10] Burns' article, guaranteed to annoy the Left, stated that 'Fascism is Left Wing' and went on:

> Fascism is not right wing; it is a form of socialism involving the same commitment to a state-controlled economy and society. The National Front, Hitler, Mussolini, or the South African government cannot accurately be described as 'right-wing', because any law which discriminates against a particular race or religion is an infringement of individual freedom.[11]

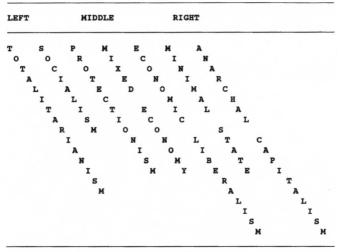

Figure 4.2 Political Spectrum

Concluding with a critique of contemporary British Conservatism, Burns asserted:

> Conservatism is nothing more than the preservation of the *status quo*. As such it is capable of lying anywhere on the political spectrum. The most conservative party in British politics is currently the Labour Party. As Robin Cook, Labour's health spokesman, recently admitted: 'It is the Labour Party, not the Conservative Party, which constantly surfaces to defend the status quo and vested interests under threat.'
> The Conservative Party, with its commitment to a semi-free-market economy, lies slightly to the right of centre.
> British politics is, however, confused by the fact that for a long time the Conservative Party represented the Establishment. There are, therefore, still many Conservatives who are attracted to the State's traditional role of controlling people's social lives. The corollary is also true because the previously anti-establishment, Labour Party, despite being firmly to the left with its economic policies, is seen as the champion of civil liberties. It was a Labour government, for example, which legalised homosexuality.[12]

In the SCCF's second magazine article, by Kim Henry, entitled 'Authoritarianism: The Moral Right', the reader was advised to 'REJECT AUTHORITARIANISM AND BACK THE MARKET'.[13] Henry launched a vehement attack on authoritarian (statist) Conservatives by arguing that:

> Authoritarians do not place a high value on the market as a guarantor of individual liberty, and are much more interested in developing ideas about the State as a symbol of political identity, the nature of nationalism, the role of religion in political solidarity. Their work represents a major theoretical attack on individualist liberalism which they believe to be alien to the Conservative instinct ... Classical Liberals within our movement are often rebuked for rocking the boat, or, in some cases 'hijacking the Party'. Yet, we don't apologise for the fact that, to their own electoral advantage, the Conservatives have managed to accommodate many shades of political opinion.[14]

After this brief conciliatory note Henry goes on to conclude: 'The authoritarians' commitment to the market is limited. Yet, they have stolen some of our language, incorporated it successfully into their doctrine, and are using it for their own hypocritical and disgusting purposes.'[15]

By 1990 Conservative student publications were so radical and outspoken they had become virtually indistinguishable from those produced by the FCS. Scottish Conservative Student's spring term *Capitalist Worker* was typical of the Libertarianism being articulated. As well as incorporating the popular Conservative student views that 'Students Want an End to the Union Closed Shop'[16] and 'Fascism is left-wing',[17] this publication argued that with regard to the conjunction of high interest rates and the ambulance drivers' strike for higher pay:

> Any mortgage payer should think twice before chucking coins into the ambulance drivers' begging bowls.
>
> It is they, after all, with their inflationary pay claims who could prevent interest rates from coming down sooner rather than later.
>
> Of course, there would be no problem if interest rates were set by the high street banks and building societies rather than the Chancellor. Interest rates are all about cash flow. If a bank needs more money it has to put up interest rates. In this country, however, it is the Government which decides when banks need more money!
>
> *SCS says stop interfering with the market Mr Major, Abolish the Bank of England.*[18]

CCF ideology is clearly similar to that found in the FCS. Yet, their style of activism is very different. While today's Conservative students regard themselves as ideologically 'sound', they display little of the FCS's capacity for mischief. In an attempt to avoid damaging press coverage, the movement has put far more emphasis on public relations. Media courses and discussion groups have been set up and pamphlets circulated in an attempt to raise the CCF's media profile and pacify CCO. A typical example of the material produced was released in early 1990 by SCCF's press officer Clive Schmulian. In the *Media Training Guide* he wrote:

> The Conservative Party are terrified of a return to the FCS headlines as seen during the mid-eighties and now make every effort to keep Conservative Students and journalists as far apart as possible.
>
> This guide provides many examples of positive headlines created by student activists, proving the error of the Party's negative approach to Conservative students and the media.[19]

Schmulian's media guide did not advocate the toning down of ideology, he simply argued that such views should be sensitively packaged for public consumption. 'Case study #1' read, for instance:

> Summary: Nelson Mandela football team linked to the murder of 14 year-old Stompi Moketsi – alleged involvement of Mrs Winnie Mandela. Glasgow University Conservatives demand immediate resignation of Mrs Mandela, who is the Rector of the University.
>
> Media strategy: (i) News conference held in conjunction with Conservatives Against Apartheid – notification faxed to media.
> (ii) Letter demanding resignation sent to Mrs Mandela – copy faxed to media.
> (iii) Details of story sent to news agency in RSA.
>
> Coverage obtained: Glasgow Herald, Scotsman, Glasgow Evening Times, Daily Record, The Sun, Daily Express, South African Press, Glasgow University Guardian, local newspapers. STV – Scottish Questions – interview (live) with Anti-Apartheid Movement – BBC TV news bulletin – BBC Radio Scotland news bulletins – Radio Clyde news bulletins.
>
> Conservative Party reaction: 100% support for Conservative Students!!
>
> Analysis: Extensive positive coverage obtained, successful news conference. For the first time in years the left at Glasgow University didn't know what had hit them.[20]

In six other similar cases referred to in the *Media Training Guide* the underlying message was clear, be 'sound' but don't rock the boat. Covering a range of campaign successes, including Glasgow University Conservatives demolishing a mock Berlin Wall, a campaign against the NUS, and a protest against a visit to Scotland by the Socialist President of Nicaragua, Daniel Ortega, the Guide showed how well thought out media plans could attract sympathetic publicity for radical free-market causes.[21]

4.2 The 'Liberation' of the Young Conservatives

With the closure of the FCS, media attention quickly moved to the possibility of ex-FCS activists encouraging Libertarianism within the

YCs. At the time, the wet YC national chairman Richard Fuller argued that CCO did not fully appreciate the nature of the Libertarian threat and asserted:

> Closing down FCS is not enough. They will move in on the YC's; if they close down the YC's, they will move into the trade union organisation, then the women, then the Parliamentary Party. What is Central Office going to do then? Close down the Parliamentary Party?[22]

As has been mentioned above, there is evidence that a number of Libertarians moved straight from the FCS into the YCs. However, a substantial number had never belonged to, nor had any contact with, the FCS. They had little knowledge of groups like the Libertarian Alliance or the Adam Smith Institute. Instead, many had been exposed to Libertarian ideas first through the writings of authors such as Adam Smith, Frederick Hayek and Milton Friedman before leaving school and entering higher education. During the early 1980s these authors began to become widely accessible to younger students.[23] The progression of Libertarian ideas in the YCs, therefore, was not simply the result of militant entryism on the part of some ex-FCS activists, but also of a spontaneous ideological shift occurring at grass roots level.

Nevertheless, from the time of the FCS's closure the prospect of a Libertarian takeover of the YCs haunted both the wets and CCO. Believing strongly in a 'militant entryist/conspiracy theory' it was not long before CCO began a new internal enquiry into the antics of Libertarian activists in the YCs. Under the heading 'Tories probe "loony" Right revenge plot' Peter Dobbie of the *Mail on Sunday* noted:

> Senior Tories are holding an inquiry into their own Militant Tendency.
> Fears that the 'loony' Right of the party is preparing a coup to take over the Young Conservatives has led to a secret investigation within Central Office.
> ... The row is set to boil over at Eastbourne. With no election in the offing, and the absence of Mrs Thatcher from the Conference, organisers fear that Right wingers will hound ministers and shout down speakers.
> YC Chairman Nick Robinson said: 'There is a cancer in our ranks that we must get rid of.'[24]

1987–88 saw war break out within the YCs. As Libertarians began to take firm control of a number of key regions senior wets found that they were coming under increasing attack. That year's *Report of the Representatives* from the Greater London Young Conservatives (GLYC) to the National Advisory Committee (NAC) demonstrates the emerging hostility. Under the heading 'MEETINGS' the report began:

At the beginning of the year the GLYC representatives had felt Mr Robinson's period as National YC Chairman could not fail to be better than that of his unpopular predecessor. These hopes were dashed at the outset, although Mr Robinson's marginally more tolerant chairing of NAC meetings allowed these occasions to rise somewhat from the depths of incivility achieved over the previous year. However, the NAC remained a place where decisions taken by the National Officers and their secret caucus were rubber-stamped and any opposition, however constructive, was brushed aside and scorned. GLYC is acknowledged as being in the vanguard of those areas prepared to stand up against the National Officers when we believe they are following the wrong course.[25]

Concerning an attempt by wet YC national officers to appoint Edward Heath as the movement's new Life Patron the GLYC report went on:

The representatives of most areas were shocked by the National Chairman's appointment of Edward Heath as our new Life Patron and angered by his refusal to accept the nomination of Mrs Thatcher for the post. GLYC Chairman Andrew Rosindell condemned the move as a calculated insult to the Prime Minister in the weeks before the General Election.[26]

Indicating the level of ideological in-fighting, the report concluded, under the heading 'MOTIONS':

The tenor of motions passed by the NAC continued to be un-supportive of the direction in which our Government is taking the country. The National YCs continue to emphasise issues involving high public spending on which there is little difference between Conservatives and Socialists.[27]

Although this document was a one-sided account of events it serves to demonstrate the emergence of ideologically based inter-factional hostility within the YCs on a scale that Abrams and Little (see the beginning of Chapter II) could not have imagined.

Commenting on the 1988 national YC conference at Eastbourne, Simon Heffer wrote, in the *Daily Telegraph*:

Central Office has made no secret of its fear that some hardened elements on the right will shout down some of the ministers sent to speak to the Young Conservatives Conference whom they judge ideologically 'unsound'.

No list of speakers has been finalised, but a favourite of previous conferences, Mr Peter Walker, is the leading hate figure with the Right Wingers and his inclusion could lead to some embarrassment.

Though the Party could close down the much smaller Federation of Conservative Students with little embarrassment, it is unthinkable that any such action could be taken against the Young Conservatives if they came under radical Right control.[28]

Although the 1988 conference proved to be a relatively uneventful affair, many privately claimed that the vote for national chairman had been rigged. It was rumoured that national YC officers had been left alone in the room at CCO where the ballot papers were stored and that 'irregularities' had occurred. Again, both sides were said to have registered bogus YC branches in the hope of boosting their vote. Whatever the case, the wet national YC chairman Martin Woodroofe was re-elected, beating the Libertarian candidate Andrew Tinney.

It was under wet control during 1988 that the 'Libertarianisation' of the YC movement finally took place. A stream of radical free market publications began to circulate that broke with their tradition of consensual pragmatism. Leading the way, Scottish Young Conservatives (SYC) published *Two Cheers for Ideology* by Dr Larry Briskman. In it he argued:

> The simple truth is that a free-market based social order encourages innovation and entrepreneurship, and this tends to undermine the very habits of doffing the cap and touching the forelock upon which Tory grandeeism depends – and, as Adam Smith said, in commercial society everyone is, in a sense, an entrepreneur, since even the humblest must sell themselves in the open market. Moreover, by delivering the goods of economic growth, setting people free to compete with one another for the favours of both consumers and employers, and basing social relations on contract, the liberal social order undermines the very habits of traditional dependence upon which the Tory grandee bases his claim of the 'right to rule'.
>
> ... For many older members, and even some younger members of the Party who form the High Tory school, the most disturbing element of this revolution is, as it is to T. E. Utley, the hijacking of the Tory Party itself by a band of ideologues, committed to the old Whig vision of free men in a free market: of personal independence, anti-paternalism, anti-Statism, and so on. Such members of the Party are, I am afraid, unwilling or unable to see that the traditional basis of the Party's claim of the right to govern had been mortally undermined by the success of the liberal market order. It was thus a necessity, not a temporary political aberration, that the basis of the Party's appeal to the British public became itself an ideologically based one.[29]

In the foreword to this document the national SYC chairman argued:

> It is surely time for the Scottish Conservative Party to formulate an ideology, a yardstick, against which the worth and practicality of policies should be measured. Fortunately, some steps have already been taken in this direction ... This is to be welcomed, however, a great deal more remains to be done.... . If we are to take the Socialist Republic of Scotland into a new age of enlightenment we must be armed with more than a willingness to serve Scotland. We must be willing to change it to what our beliefs tell us is right.[30]

In his opening address to the 1989 YC conference the deputy chairman of the Conservative Party, Peter Morrison, warned delegates:

For the next 48 hours, you are the Conservative Party in the minds of the television viewers and the newspaper readers. So, please, during the course of the next 48 hours make sure that the way you conduct your arguments is just as important as the substance of them.[31]

In a telling comment more appropriate for a YC conference of thirty years ago, Morrison went on:

If some of the real activists here heard me saying this they would kill me … but an awful lot of people don't want to become deeply involved in political issues. They don't want all the hassles and the deep political argument. It is a political organisation, but also an organisation where like-minded people can get together and have a bit of fun. Most young-sters want to join because they are Conservatives – they don't want to be bound up in a Punch and Judy show.[32]

Frightened of rampant factionalism, the Conservative Party approached the YC conference with trepidation. According to Helen Chappell in the *New Statesman and Society*, Cecil Parkinson began his speech by saying: 'I don't know what you do to the enemy, but by God, you terrify me.'[33] For the first time in living memory the party leader, Mrs Thatcher, snubbed the conference and refused to attend. Outlining the tensions, Robert Shrimsley wrote in the *Sunday Telegraph*:

The Prime Minister was expected, by tradition, to address the Confer-ence, and the announcement that she would not do so prompted specu-lation that she was keen to dissociate herself from some of the Young Conservatives' more embarrassing activities and factional infighting.

Mr Martin Woodroofe, the Chairman, said 'Naturally we are disap-pointed, but the Prime Minister's support and enthusiasm for the organ-isation has never been in doubt.'

Within the past month she has met both National Officers and Area Chairmen at Downing Street and the winners of our Superbranch compe-tition – hardly the actions of a Prime Minister trying to distance herself.[34]

Proving their support for Libertarian ideas, the conference voted against a motion on law and order that criticised the American 'Guardian Angels'. Against the Conservative tradition of supporting the (State) Police, one delegate, Miss Patricia Sale from mid-Bed-fordshire, told the meeting how she had been mugged on the Lon-don Underground and stated: 'We should welcome the Guardian Angels with open arms. They remind us it is our duty to be active cit-izens and not to turn our backs.'[35]

Summing up the conference, John Pienaar wrote in the *Independent*:

SOUTHPORT survived this weekend's visit by the Young Conserva-tives, and the relief showed on the faces of the Party elders from Central Office. This time, there would be no headlines about chaotic conference faction-fighting or sprees of loutish behaviour in the town. Margaret Thatcher was widely thought to have avoided the Young Conservatives'

Annual Conference on the grounds of potential embarrassment. In the end, though, the consensus seemed to be that the party's youth wing had at last cleaned up its act.

That reaction is misleading. It masks uncertainty over the Young Conservatives' influence, its traditional role as seed-bed of future MPs and concern over its now openly acknowledged problem of attracting new members.

… But perhaps of more fundamental importance is the fact that radical right-wingers at last seem confident of ousting the traditionally 'wet' leadership in the YC's postal ballot next March. Each faction is portraying the battle as a fight to preserve the organisation from extinction at the hands of the other.[36]

In an attempt to warn off the YC's from succumbing to Libertarianism, Woodroofe had argued that the radical right would simply result in extremism and embarrassment for the Party:

To Mr Woodroofe, the new right was simply a sanitised version of the FCS. At a foot-stomping rally of his supporters on Saturday night, he denounced the right, with more passion than originality, as a crowd of extremist bigots. 'Let's give the people that peddle that filth a bloody nose,' he urged. And during an appearance in the Conference Press Room, he maintained that a Tinney-led YC would quickly revert to the old ways of the disbanded and politically embarrassing FCS leadership.[37]

Woodroffe not only argued that FCS entryism was behind the rise of YC Libertarianism, but he hinted that they were now more dangerous because they were more subtle:

A lot of Tinney's supporters are not just young people going through a stage in their youth. People came from the FCS determined to take over the Young Conservatives, and some to wreck it.

This year they have agreed to behave themselves. They are keeping their heads down, speaking softly and wearing smarter suits. But they are still there. If they win, it will mean an inevitable spiral down to closure in a couple of years' time.[38]

In March 1989, the Libertarian candidate, Andrew Tinney, took over as chairman of the YCs. Although the wets had polled more votes in the vice-chairmen ballot, holding all four positions and a majority on the National Advisory Committee, they privately admitted that the result had been a disaster. Tinney's victory had given the Libertarians the triumph they had been looking for. And although the party had attempted to stop their progress, by advising the honorary officers (senior figures like Kenneth Clarke) to vote, the strategy failed.

For John Pienaar of the *Independent*, Tinney was no ordinary 'radical Thatcherite', he was a determined and robust ideologue:

During the Conference, Mr Tinney sought to play down his own right-wing views. He nevertheless managed, in the space of a few minutes at one appearance, to urge the abolition of the NHS in favour of a national insurance scheme, and to advocate the return of the death penalty by lethal injection. Victory, to him, meant ridding the Party of the 'last bastion of wetness', and standing ready to support a 'suitable' successor to Mrs Thatcher. None was visible so far, he added.[39]

Despite Tinney having won the leadership, the Libertarians had not achieved the total breakthrough on the NAC they hoped for. In reality it was left up to him to use his prominent position subtly to advance the faction's case during the following year, in the hope that it would form a majority on the national committee: a task that, as William Leith of the *Tatler* noted, Tinney was well suited for:

> Andrew can drive, talk complex free-market politics and light the Superkings he constantly smokes without missing a beat. He's sensible enough not to fall for the occasional hard-right views which I slip into the conversation. In fact his politics, the politics which appeal to his supporters, are practical rather than ideological, the kind of ideas which appeal to young, pushy, disco-going people. Surely things work better when people have a personal investment in them? Surely it's better not to penalise people just for making a lot of money? After all, making rich people poorer doesn't necessarily make poor people richer.
>
> He talks about his recent election campaign, the famous 'presidential-style' rallies he organised at the Southport Young Conservative Conference. Anybody who saw TV clips of the rallies will realise how the YC's are aiming themselves, with a certain amount of success, at a totally different kind of young person. There were cheerleaders with pom-poms and short skirts and Tinney T-shirts, there were lasers, dry ice, a customised rock soundtrack of triumphal music for when Tinney made an entrance. Posters and T-shirts and banners were colour-coded to be camera catching. Tinney wore a sharp suit and had a slight quiff. These people didn't need ad-men to tell them what to do – they could do it all for themselves. They had grown up, after all, in an age when it feels natural to merge product and promotion.[40]

Concentrating on Tinney's programme as YC chairman, Leith went on:

> Now he's trying to make his mark in the world of adult politics. He's set up two fringe meetings at the next Party Conference in September. One featured card-carrying Wet Douglas Hurd as the speaker. A clever choice this: plenty of potential high-profile conflict in the offing. The other is a debate on broadcasting which sets Tim Renton MP, keen auctioneer of TV franchises, against a nice fat Liberal target, Michael Grade. More flak, more coverage. Best of all, the YCs are publishing right-wing MP John Redwood's Popular Capitalist Manifesto. 'It's a reply to the 1848 Communist Manifesto,' says Andrew. 'We hope to translate it into six languages.[41]

Throughout 1989 Tinney walked a political tight-rope. He adhered to many of the radical policies favoured by his supporters whilst also obtaining positive media coverage and the support of CCO. He had transformed the YCs into a radical political organisation. Commenting on his first year in office Tinney's campaign manager John Swannick proudly stated: 'Years ago the YC's was nothing much more than a marriage bureau, a nice social club. Nowadays we are a dynamic, businesslike organisation.'[42]

At the 1990 national YC conference Tinney and the Libertarian slate won a majority on the national committee. Covering the conference for the *Financial Times* Ralph Atkins wrote:

> This year saw an attempt at a damage limitation exercise by Conservative Central Office. The aim was to stop the loutish behaviour, division and head-line-grabbing extremism that has marred previous Conferences.
>
> ... The operation, however, was only partly successful. There were no embarrassing outrages and the police reported a quiet Saturday night. But the colourful in-fighting that has split the YC's and might threaten its future continued unabated.
>
> The dispute, for aficionados, centres on two factions. In the ascendancy is 'The Right Team,' led by YC Chairman Mr Andrew Tinney ...
>
> Arch-rival to Mr Tinney is Mr Laurence Harris, a 24-year-old trainee solicitor, representing a more moderate wing and standing to be next year's Chairman ...
>
> Rivalry between the two factions is deadly. Mr Harris was booed when he chaired the Conference. Mr Tinney was accused of raising massive campaign funds from dubious sources.
>
> Journalists need not dig for slurs and innuendo – both present it in press releases.
>
> The election hustings session was marked by slow hand clapping, stormy protests, angry speeches, hissing and booing – all in rich quantities.[43]

Although during his first year in office Tinney had developed a good working relationship with CCO, the 1990 conference highlighted the gulf that remained between the YCs and many of the party's senior figures. According to Ralph Atkins:

> Mrs Thatcher and her Cabinet colleagues appeared to look on the YC's with the eyes of bemused parents who believe they should control their offspring but are not sure how. The Prime Minister was patronising. 'I'm afraid you are asking such deep questions that each of them is taking up a little speech of their own,' she said as she fended off questions about local government finance.
>
> Mr Kenneth Baker, national party chairman, told his audience 'your task – and your only task – is to go out together and fight Socialism.'[44]

Given what had gone before, the Libertarian victory in the YCs had been entirely predictable. The systematic takeover of the FCS and the CCF, the gradual permeation of a growing number of YC branches and areas, and the considerable ability and marketability of 'Tinney's Team' all provided for a conjunction of forces that made the Libertarian triumph a logical conclusion.

4.3   Takeover: The Mechanics of Libertarian Permeation.

In order to understand the takeover by Libertarians of the Conservative Party's youth groups it is important to analyse their organisational structures and their different electoral systems. For while Libertarianism influenced many activists in the FCS, the CCF and the YCs, it is important to recognise that it gained ground in a variety of constitutional settings that themselves had a major impact on its development.

The electoral system of the Federation of Conservative Students was almost designed for factional politics. Each branch had to submit a membership list to the permanent secretary of the Federation who would then authorise branch representation to the annual conference in proportion to the size of the membership of that branch.

Libertarian activists determined to achieve national dominance had three basic and distinct ways to progress. The first usually carried out in a new or small FCS branch, was to boost membership artificially. This was done either through 'associate membership' or through what was known as the 'telephone directory' method. The former involves granting membership to students without charge but officially with their knowledge and agreement. At one polytechnic any student who at any time had attended an branch function, such as a disco or a speaker meeting, was automatically awarded 'Associate Membership' for the duration of their stay at the polytechnic. So a fresher who had attended a debate with the Labour Students could in theory have been recorded as a member for as long as four years without any further participation. Although this particular example was a 'wet' dominated branch, such practices crossed factional lines.

Registering non-existent students or non-Conservatives was known as the 'Telephone Directory' method and depended for its success on the difficulty for CCO in verifying membership claims given the absence of a Central Office agent on the spot. The absence of senior Party control at a local level goes a long way towards explaining the openness with which Libertarians could present themselves in internal elections.

The second route for Libertarians in the FCS was the takeover of individual 'enemy' branches. Here the competing factions would lobby for support, recruit extra members and attempt to ensure maximum supporter turnout when necessary. Elections in these branches were fought on a slate basis, with the winner seizing control of all the major offices, particularly Chairman and secretary. The victorious faction would then often privately allocate tickets to the FCS national conference, preferring to 'forget' to fill all the places rather than allow 'unsound' people to have voting rights.

The third and most outwardly apparent method of increasing Libertarian influence within the FCS was achieved via 'creative branch registration'. This involved the establishment of an FCS branch in a college where none existed previously and in many cases in colleges where a campus life was non-existent. Examples of this technique would be found in the further education colleges where a branch could be set up by a part-time 'O' Level student or in a secretarial, or even Sixth Form, college. The loose definition of a student offered by the NAC's rules, which included anyone enrolled on a 'Department of Education and Science approved course', meant that many abuses of the spirit of the rules were possible. However, perhaps the most extreme example of rule bending for the Party must surely have been the transgression of the geographical boundaries set by the party's National Union. This involved the registration of collegiate branches in Northern Ireland, making the FCS the only section of the Conservative Party to operate in that province.

The alliance of the Libertarians to the cause of supporting Ulster membership was founded on a number of tactical as well as ideological grounds. The Ulster contingent at FCS conferences, normally closely aligned to the right-wing Scottish group, was 'sound' on the 'Liberation struggle against the IRA', and, most important of all, by their very presence, an embarrassment to the 'soft' CCO observers and the party faithful. The subsequent campaign for Conservative organisation in Northern Ireland was the logical outcome of FCS branches in Ulster colleges, when departing students could not then join local Conservative Associations. It is interesting that most opposition to the campaign came from the same quarters who within the FCS had opposed Libertarianism and the desire to allow FCS branches to be registered in Northern Ireland.[45]

Unlike Oxford and Cambridge with their collegiate structures and tradition of paternalistic Toryism, which made them virtually inaccessible to Libertarian takeover, it is worth noting that the newer colleges, where FCS branches did not exist or did not have a long established history were the ones where Libertarians were most able to create or take over a branch. In the FCS there was a perception of an ideological and sociological divide between the 'red-brick' and 'sandstone' colleges, the former popularly thought of as 'sound' and upwardly mobile working-class, the latter 'wet' and traditionally middle-class. However, such factional rivalry was, in reality, contradicted by comparison. For instance, while Oxbridge, the LSE and Kingston Polytechnic were all 'wet', St Andrews and Kings College London were 'sound'. Under analysis, it seems that class cleavages were not discernible at inter-college level, with the exception of Oxford and Cambridge.[46] The popular identification of Libertarians and Heathites on a class basis reflects more upon the relative ease with which Libertarians could take over Warwick University, compared with the more complex situation at Oxford, than on class politics.

Whereas in an FCS branch a chairman controlled a number of votes, in the YCs a branch chairman is the only person entitled to vote (along with area and national officers) in the national elections. The result of this system is that it reduces the benefit of takeovers from being a block gain to a mere net switch of two votes. Furthermore, instead of a conference vote, the electoral college votes by post – with resulting differences in turnout and factional discipline.

During the mid-1980s the emphasis for Libertarians in the YCs was directed towards the launching, or relaunching, of branches in parliamentary constituencies where no organised YC branch existed. 'Notorious' Libertarians however often encountered the obstacle of having to keep in contact with the local parliamentary Conservative Association. Where a full-time agent was employed, this involved possible monitoring by CCO and occasional intervention. Initially therefore YC branches were only taken over where they were weak or defunct and often by Libertarians who consciously toned down their views for local party consumption. Although a few YC branches were initially taken over, most of the 'sound' ones were set up in defunct areas. For instance, in 1987 Greater London Area had the potential for eighty-four branches, yet at the time there were only seventy-five active Conservative Associations and seventy YC branches.

As in the FCS, once a YC area was taken over the offices of chairman and secretary were ruthlessly used to disqualify 'accidentally' enemy branches by such devices as the sending of branch registration forms to the wrong address and often too late to count anyway. Because both sides used this tactic CCO established clearer rules that were harder to abuse. However, their action came too late, closing the stable door after the horse had bolted. A sound branch could use out-of-date members or shared members with other branches to qualify using the loop-hole of 'residence, employment or a historic connection with the constituency'. Furthermore, a determined YC branch chairman could get an agent (grateful for the auxiliary help in elections) to allow practically anyone to join on the flimsiest of qualifications. CCO rules hit branches run by chairmen who were not fanatical about branch registration and political campaigns: the natural wet. By the time the rules were introduced in 1989 not only had the FCS Libertarians set up their branches but they had long since handed over to their deputies, many of whom had no FCS record whatsoever, making a crack down impossible.

To a considerable extent, the infiltration of Libertarians into the FCS was far more overt than it was into the YCs. On matters of foreign policy, terrorism and privatisation, Libertarian YCs showed their colours. On the other hand it would take considerable effort to locate any evidence that they supported the legalisation of prostitution and drug taking and the abolition of compulsory education. This is not to say, however, that such views had been renounced, they were simply driven underground. The Libertarians appear to have learned from the far left the art of 'discreet entryism'.

The CCF experience was similar to that of the YCs. Here again, so far as CCO action on curbing Libertarianism went it was often either too little and too late or simply misguided, based on the false assumption of massive militant infiltration. CCO too readily associated the somewhat dubious activities of Libertarian electioneering with CCF (and the YCs) with the FCS's second generation. Although these individuals most certainly did have a role to play, the bulk of these activities were carried out spontaneously by 'third-generation' youngsters – and often to the surprise and amusement of their ex-FCS elders.

Although CCO wanted more control over the CCF, and therefore decided to appoint its regional and national officers directly, after the demise of FCS talent was hard to come by. As time went on it became apparent that people were being appointed to positions irrespective of their political opinions. For CCO found itself choosing individuals on the basis of their simply being prepared to 'do a job'. As a result of the vacuum created by the closure of the FCS, a small number of hard-working Libertarians were thus able to obtain party approval and soon found themselves in a number of high-ranking positions.

Therefore, while there is evidence that a number of ex-FCS activists influenced the subsequent Libertarianisation of the NACG, the CCF and the YCs (by either joining them directly and thus working from the inside, or working informally from the outside) this is by no means the whole story. The rise of Libertarian ideas after 1986 cannot simply be attributed to the factor of FCS entryism, but has to be understood in the context of specific constitutional environments and, to some extent, as the spontaneous result of a grass-roots movement reflecting wider socio-political trends.

Notes and References

1. In October 1986 the Party Chairman withdrew CCO facilities and financial support from the National Committee of the FCS. He appointed the Conservative Collegiate Forum under the chairmanship of the Hon. Peter Morrison, MP, and John Bercow was appointed vice-chairman. On 15 April 1987 the National Executive Committee dissolved the FCS. The new CCF committee included ex-FCS activist Simon McVicker as vice-chairman.

2. It is interesting to note that the Conservative conference handbook issued in Blackpool October 1987 read: 'The growth in membership of the Association last year signalled a continuation of the revival in fortunes of the Conservative Graduates, with membership up by over 40% since 1985. By providing a focal point for recent graduates, NACG forms an important link for politically active students in their transition from university to active constituency participation.' No doubt many of the NACG's new 'politically active students' were ex-FCS members repositioning themselves in the party structure. See: *104th Conservative Conference Handbook*, London, National Union of Conservative and Unionist Associations, p. 115.

3. 'Conservative Students' was founded by a small group of radical free-market students in direct response to the closure of the FCS. Its primarily worked with 'sound' Conservative student branches thought to be threatened by the party. It produced a variety of posters, badges, and publications.

4. Quote from an ex-FCS student at a London polytechnic who wishes to remain anonymous.

5. 'Long March for the loony right', *7 Days Perspective*, 21 February 1987, p. 7.

6. Tony Clark, 'Young tories fund Contra terrorists', *Morning Star*, 11 July 1987.

7. London Conservative Students, *1988 Defenders of Liberty Handbook*, London, Greater London Area Conservative Collegiate Forum, p. 30.

8. Burns, M., 'Who's Right', *The Scottish Conservative Collegiate Forum 1989 Conference Magazine*, p. 4.

9. Ibid.

10. Ibid.

11. Ibid., p. 5.

12. Ibid.

13. Ibid., p. 7.

14. Ibid., p. 6.

15. Ibid., p. 7.

16. Scottish Conservative Students (1990) *Capitalist Worker*, Spring Term, p. 1.

17. Ibid., p. 4.

18. Ibid., p. 2.

19. Scottish Conservative Students, (1990) *Media Training Guide*, p. 1.

20. Ibid., p. 3.

21. Ibid. See also: *Glasgow Herald*, 29 September 1989; *Scotsman*, 6 October 1989; *Scotsman*, 5 October 1989; *Evening Times*, 21 May 1989; *Scotsman*, 20 January 1990; *Glasgow Herald*, 20 January 1990; *Daily Express*, 20 January 1990; *The Sun*, 20 January 1990; *Daily Record*, 20 January 1990; *Scotsman*, 6 June 1989; *Scotsman*, 18 January 90; *Scotsman*, 31 March 1989; *Scottish Daily Express*, 27 November 1989.

22. 'Young Tories rampaging through party sensibilities', *Guardian*, 9 February 1987.

23. The IEA's journal, *Economic Affairs*, has for some years targeted A-Level economics students.

24. Dobbie, P., 'Tories probe "loony" Right revenge plot', *Mail on Sunday*, 3 January 1988.

25. Greater London Young Conservatives (1988) *GLYC Report of the Representatives to the National Advisory Committee*.

26. Ibid.

27. Ibid.

28. Heffer, S., *Daily Telegraph*, 8 February 1988.
29. Briskman, L., (1988) *Two Cheers For Ideology*, Edinburgh, Scottish Young Conservatives, pp. 10–11.
30. Ibid., p. 6.
31. Craig, J., 'Young Tories show they mean business', *Sunday Times*, 12 February 1989, p. 2.
32. Pienaar, J., 'Young Tories change their spots', *Independent*, 13 February 1989, p. 19.
33. Chappell, H., 'Young blue bloods', *New Statesman and Society*, 17 February 1989, p. 15.
34. Shrimsley, R., 'Young Tories deny No 10 snub', *Sunday Telegraph*, 12 February 1989, p. 5.
35. *Sunday Times*, 12 February 1989, p. 2.
36. *Independent*, 13 February 1989, p. 19.
37. Ibid.
38. Ibid.
39. Ibid. Tinney's apparent support for the death penalty resembles the coalition building tactics used by early Libertarians in the FCS to gain an electoral majority with the aid of authoritarian support. It is questionable whether he really believed in such a policy.
40. 'Know Your Rights', *Tatler*, September 1989, Volume 284, No. 8, p. 116.
41. Ibid.
42. *Sunday Times*, 11 February 1990, p. A–9.
43. *Financial Times*, 12 February 1990, p. 6.
44. *Financial Times*, 12 February 1990, p. 6.
45. It is noticeable that wet Conservative students at Oxford and Cambridge universities also opposed the establishment of Conservative Party associations in Northern Ireland.
46. Paradoxically, Oxford and Cambridge Conservative Associations only really embraced radical free-market ideas after the FCS had been closed down. Because they had strong union societies separate from the NUS, and a tradition of 'institutionalised Toryism', the student environment was very different from that found in other universities. Conservative Students were not threatened by a powerful hard left and consequently had less cause to embrace Libertarian ideas.

ఆ Chapter V ౨

THE SOCIAL BACKGROUND AND DEGREE OF LIBERTARIANISM WITHIN CONSERVATIVE PARTY YOUTH STRUCTURES

5.1   Introduction to the Quantitative Enquiry

Given the evidence presented, it is plausible to imagine that under analysis the youth wings of the Conservative Party would demonstrate strong Libertarian tendencies. It can be expected that in terms of social and political values there exists today a substantial intergenerational cleavage between the Party's older and younger members.

The quantitative research undertaken, therefore, had two primary goals. Firstly, it was designed to profile the sociological and ideological nature of the party's youth. In particular, to detect any correlation between their views and such social factors as class or religious belief. Secondly, it attempted to profile older members' views so that an ideological comparison with the younger generation could be made.

However, because the Conservative Party was understandably sensitive about such research (not least for reasons of individual confidentiality), it was not possible for the author to obtain official membership lists and thereby examine a 'perfect' sample. Nevertheless, the research compiled is from an accurate and representative sample of branch, regional, area and national 'activists' (as opposed to the ordinary members), as the author was able to attend many YC branch, CCF branch, CCF training, CCF conference, and NACG

Notes for this section begin on page 125.

events. It is estimated that out of the party's total youth movement the author questioned around four per cent of the combined membership. In terms of the 'activists' this figure is probably nearer seventy per cent and of the national officers eighty per cent. Although it could be argued that a representative sample of the whole membership would have been more desirable, the history of other political youth movements suggests it is the 'core activists' who are important. For it is they who are elected to represent their members and from whom tomorrow's politicians tend to emerge.[1]

Early pilot studies indicated the complex nature of Libertarian politics. The simple question: 'Should the government sell off British Rail?' for example, created surprising problems for a number of respondents. While believing passionately in private enterprise, many answered 'no', interpreting a 'yes' as countenancing the transference of private capital into state hands. They could not sanction privatisation because it would raise money for the state. Question wording was not the only area in which problems presented themselves. Because of the difficulty in obtaining national membership lists and the understandable sensitivity of many respondents, a short self-completion questionnaire was finally deemed to be the most suitable means of data collection.

From the outset, respondents were told that the information gathered was for a thesis analysing the Conservative Party and throughout the process its serious nature was stressed. The respondents were assured that their anonymity would be guaranteed at all times and that even their branch names would not be revealed.

To conduct the research among older Conservatives, a number of associations were chosen at random in different parts of the country.[2] The questions asked were identical to those for the young. The research was conducted between October 1990 and April 1991. The sample of 455 respondents included 174 senior party members and 281 young party members.

When filling in the questionnaires respondents were not allowed to talk to or confer with each other. It was made clear that what was wanted was their own views. To this end, 'don't know' (DK) options were not included because, as Schuman and Presser advise, in a survey like this which is interested in people's underlying dispositions, it is better to encourage a definite 'one way or the other' response by not providing a 'get-out'.[3] If respondents did not understand a question they were told to leave it blank.

The results were evaluated using a number of statistical tools. Tables 5.1 to 5.3 display the assessment by the survey population of eight political leaders. For this purpose an 'unsoundness percentage' was constructed. The respondent was invited to mark on a scale of 1 to 8 a choice of eight leaders. If all repondents had rated one person as a '1' then the total would be 281. For a universal rating of '8' the total would be 2248. The average was calculated by dividing the total by 2248. The unsoundness percentage was calculated by rebasing the figures (i.e. for 'Thatcher': 433 minus 281, divided by 2248 minus 281, multiplied by 100).

Tables 5.4 to 5.8, 5.10 and 5.11 are simple percentage tables. For Tables 5.8 and 5.9, also for the Segregation Index relating to Class (Appendix I, Section A), the categories were compiled from the UCCA Report for 1988-89 and the OPCS. Table 5.9 is more complex because it involves the calculation of a percentage variation for class. Segregation index tables have been added in Appendix I. These were calculated by adding the absolute values of the variations between two samples, and halving the sum.

Given the subject matter and the constraints on undertaking the research, it was inevitable that the quantitative data achieved would have to be interpreted and contextualised – to some extent. However, given the powerful results achieved, it is only fair to say that the explanations provided are not a matter of subjective, personal opinion, but instead accurately reflect the ideological and social paradigm under analysis.

5.2   The Degree of Libertarianism within Conservative Party Youth Structures: An Inter-Generational Analysis

The popularly accepted paradigm view of what it means to be an 'extreme right-winger' includes the prediction that, faced with the choice of political figures listed in Table 5.1, the Libertarian contingent in the population surveyed would rate them on a 'sound/unsound' axis.

Table 5.1 Traditional Sound/Un-Sound Axis

Sound							Un-sound
HITLER	BOTHA	PINOCHET	THATCHER	HESELTINE	HEATH	GORBACHEV	BENN

The survey question presented to the youth population was headed 'Sound and Un-Sound' with the candidates listed in alphabetical order and accompanied by an invitation to represent the politicians on a scale from 1 to 8: 1 being the 'soundest' and 8 the 'unsoundest'.

From the evidence outlined in previous chapters, the Libertarian paradigm would suggest that the 'Sound/Un-Sound' axis shown in Table 5.2 might be a more accurate representation of the anarchic tendencies of Libertarians:[4]

Table 5.2 Libertarian Sound/Un-Sound Axis

Sound					Un-Sound
THATCHER	PINOCHET	HESELTINE	GORBACHEV/BOTHA	HEATH/BENN	HITLER

Whereas Adorno's research on authoritarianism and the right could be interpreted as suggesting that Hitler was in some sense sound, to the Libertarian right he is an extreme collectivist. For them, National Socialism measures people according to such collective criteria as race, sex, class and genetic health. Nazism is founded upon three 'unsound' philosophical principles: the worship of unreason, the demand for self-sacrifice, and the elevation of society above the individual.[5] Pinochet is not harshly regarded by Libertarians in so far as he is not a racist. He overthrew a 'Communist' regime, lowered taxes massively, privatised over a third of the land and adopted monetarist policies with such success that Chile's inflation and debt situation were vastly preferable to those experienced elsewhere in Latin America. For the FCS the persecution of 'communists' is not the same as the persecution of members of an ethnic minority because they argue that being a Communist is a matter of volition.

The actual results in Table 5.3 for the overall youth population surveyed provides a result very close to that anticipated by a Libertarian analysis. Given that a number of wets have undoubtedly used their left/right view, coupled with their factional preferences to give Heseltine and Heath a more respectable showing than might otherwise have been the case, the only real surprise is the poor rating of General Pinochet. Despite the general acceptance by the Conservative Party's Libertarians of the 'Kirkpatrick Doctrine',[6] which would make Pinochet a 'fellow traveller', and the combative propaganda of the FCS, the Chilean dictator polled badly. In this case it is worth pointing out that the actual result resembles the projected Libertarian view to a far greater degree than the traditional left/right one. One might even say that Pinochet suffers from being associated with State-sponsored terror. Certainly his proximity with Hitler and his distance from Thatcher is not consistent with the view that the Libertarians represent an authoritarian project. If Pinochet and Thatcher's positions were reversed, then the definition of a sound/un-sound paradigm would be truly confused!

Table 5.3 Sound or Un-Sound Results

Sound Name	THATCHER	HESELTINE	GORBACHEV	BOTHA	HEATH	PINOCHET	BENN	Un-Sound HITLER
Total	433	1079	1259	1390	1472	1550	1699	1907
Average	1.5	3.8	4.5	4.9	5.2	5.5	5.8	6.8
Un-Soundness (%)	7.7	40.6	49.7	56.4	60.6	64.6	69.0	82.7

Mrs Thatcher's rating at one-fifth of Michael Heseltine's on the 'unsoundness' scale is remarkable given the near parity of many of the other scores. Hitler's unpopularity was mitigated because his score was moderated by a desire to emphasise disapproval for other candidates (i.e. Heath). This should be read not as support for authoritarianism but considered in the context of what are known within the youth wings as 'inverse dialectics': factional in-fighting. The point to be emphasised is that these responses include those of some traditional Conservatives and young activists who support the Tory Reform Group. Even so it is clear that the paradigm of sound/un-sound is at least partly accepted by these non-Libertarian elements: a case of agenda setting by the Libertarians.

To specify the degree of the youth population's Libertarianisation, respondents were asked questions on (a) their social attitudes and (b) their economic preferences. In both sections issues were chosen that would demarcate responses of a moral and ideological nature. The degree of acceptance of a majority of the issues would be a useful indicator as to the extent of Libertarian permeation within the youth wings. The different levels of support and opposition for the various issues might make it possible to judge whether this movement is economically liberal, socially liberal, or both. It is worth pointing out that some of the proposals are not exclusively Libertarian: legalisation of Sunday trading, abortion, and international free migration and the privatisation of the monarchy, are in different ways acceptable policies to many individuals from a variety of political persuasions.

In the Table of Legalisations (Table 5.4) the issues are clear cut, freedom of choice versus social control, with the two exceptions of abortion (where opposite applications of the rights to life, liberty, and property are consistent with Libertarianism) and to an extent Sunday trading, where the issue is diluted with the problem of restrictions on shopping during leisure time (opposing serious theists and trade union officials to people unconcerned with strict religious observance, or willing to work or shop on Sundays).

Table 5.4 Table of Legalisations

Do you believe in the legalisation of ... ?

	Youth				Senior			
	Yes	(%)	**No**	(%)	**Yes**	(%)	**No**	(%)
Abortion	203	72	67	23	95	54	69	39
Prostitution	170	60	102	36	46	26	117	67
Surrogate Motherhood	178	63	89	31	20	11	141	81
Fire-Arm Possession	111	39	161	57	18	10	147	84
Homosexuality	185	65	84	29	53	30	109	62
Lesbianism	186	66	84	29	40	22	119	68
Sunday Trading	226	80	48	17	94	54	70	40
Ticket Touting	178	63	91	32	19	10	146	83
Cannabis	137	48	136	48	18	10	145	83
Heroin	89	31	184	65	7	4	156	89
Selling Human Organs	121	43	143	50	13	7	150	86

For the thesis to be substantiated, it would be necessary for the following criterion to apply: the scores in favour of legalisation of the eleven issues on offer to the youth population ought to be substantially higher in most, if not all cases, than for the corresponding scores for the senior population. Furthermore, one would expect those issues where the law was currently most prohibitive to be supported by the more committed Libertarians, whereas homosexuality being currently legal in many cases might get support because its criminalisation would involve a programme of change – something traditional Conservatives are supposed to shy from at the best of times.

On the subject of privatisation it is worth noting that at the time of research none of the nine proposed flotations had been accepted by the Conservative Government; some had been ruled out – 'The National Health Service is safe in our hands' – and others would be inconceivable at any time in the history of the party: the monarchy, the legal system, and money. British Rail, the Post Office, and the BBC would be within the realms of radical discussion and therefore might be expected to command some extensive support. The others were the quasi-exclusive agenda of the Libertarians, having been extensively discussed in the Conservative Party's youth wings, a wide range of Libertarian literature, and the free-market think-tanks.

The legalisation of the international free migration of capital and property (Table 5.7) are essentially tools of measuring the extent of internationalism as opposed to nationalism within the various groups. Whilst it may be excessive to correlate support for international free migration of labour with a non-racist world-view, it is inconsistent simultaneously to abolish immigration controls and hold a 'little Englander' view.[7]

Table 5.5 Capital Punishment

Do you believe in the restoration of Capital Punishment?

	Yes	(%)	No	(%)	No Response	(%)
Youth	114	41	156	56	11	4
Senior	80	46	76	44	18	10

On the subject of the death penalty (Table 5.5) the figures are startling in that a majority does not appear to support capital punishment among the Conservative Party as a whole and, more surprising still, only 41 per cent of the Conservative youth population surveyed supports the death penalty. A large number of factors may be responsible for this result. The greater tolerance for the right of life in Libertarians compared with traditional Conservatives may explain the 5 per cent gap between old and young. However, the context of a review of the life sentences given to the Birmingham Six and the presence also in the sample of wets who may abhor the death penalty as simply 'barbaric', cannot be ignored. At other times, it might be possible to draw definite conclusions from the death penalty figures.

On the subject of abortion the figures of 72 per cent in favour and 23 per cent against among the youth are more decisive than one might expect. The 54 per cent in favour of abortion among the senior population (joint most favoured of the eleven issues) reflects the current situation of the Conservative Party generally which is not decisive: both moves to liberalise and moves to restrict abortion are widely popular within the party.

On prostitution a clear majority, 60 per cent, support legalisation. Among the old, two-thirds oppose it but intriguingly 26 per cent are in favour. From open-ended pilot studies it was apparent that the senior respondents saw the issue as one of 'openness' and 'control' versus 'underground' and 'unchecked', the latter being the practical consequence of criminalisation. It would be fair to say that the young supporters of legalised prostitution supported for individualist, rather than 'social good' reasons.

Surrogate motherhood was supported by 63 per cent of the youth but only 11 per cent of the senior population. A combination of 'our bodies to ourselves feminism' with the virtue of entrepreneurship explains the degree of support by the young; on the part of the old the technology involved might be the source of rejection.

Firearm possession provided the first real shock. For all the restrictions, it must be said that firearm possession is still legal in the UK. That both old and young populations should therefore oppose it is somewhat surprising given the previous results. The level of support at 39 per cent is at odds with the image projected by both the traditional shotgun-toting shire Tory and the machine-gun toting 'Rambo' of FCS propaganda (see Chapter III). In reality, the idea of legitimately holding weapons for self-defence does not appear to be much favoured: perhaps a legacy of the Hungerford massacre which took place in August 1987.

Homosexuality both male and female is firmly accepted by Conservative youth but equally firmly opposed by the party's senior members (see Table 5.4). The low level of sexual toleration among senior Conservatives might be explained as being restricted to those with personal acquaintance of homosexuals or the practice of homosexuality.

Sunday trading is overwhelmingly supported by the young (80 per cent) with lukewarm support among the senior members (54 per cent). This result hints at a religious cleavage, as well as a generational one. It is an issue which has a similar profile to the 1988 debate surrounding the extension of public-house opening hours.[8]

Ticket touting appears to be associated with 'foul' crime among the senior members (10 per cent support), possibly because of recent publicity about forged tickets. Among the young the approval rating is identical to that for surrogate motherhood (63 per cent), in line with the view that they are legitimate market operations.

Cannabis and heroin produced different results amongst the different categories. Heroin has the least support among the old (4 per cent) and the young (31 per cent); still eight times more popular among the latter. Cannabis however is 'only' as objectionable to the seniors as firearm possession, surrogate motherhood and ticket touting. It seems to be unpopular among the seniors as much because it is banned at present as because of any supposed harm it causes to society. Among the youth however, heroin is clearly regarded as harmful, more so than may be acceptable for market forces. Despite this, many opponents of heroin use favour its legalisation on the grounds that after an initial rush to experiment, its popularity would rapidly diminish along with its costs in accordance with supply-side models. Cannabis, however, is not conclusively regarded as harmful by the youth population. It is as strongly supported (48 per cent) as it is opposed (also 48 per cent). Therefore it is the most controversial legalisation issue in the sense of being the most divisive among the young.

The sale of human organs has become an issue following the discovery that it was being practised by a hospital in the UK. These circumstances led to considerable moral outrage against this practice, especially as it appeared that the donors were ignorant of the potential health hazards involved. The senior population responded accordingly by scoring 7 per cent approval for this practice despite the absence of deaths caused by the sale of human organs by live donors. Among the youth population, support was only slightly against legalisation (43 per cent for, 50 per cent against). Undoubtedly, many respondents considered it was analogous to the donor card system currently legal in the UK with the refinement of 'cash for organs'. The issue is therefore closer to one about the morality of capitalism and the ownership of our bodies, and is not simply a question of risk.

The overall picture of the legalisation table suggests that the Conservative Party would not gain majority approval among its senior members for criminalising abortion or Sunday trading, but that they support the criminalisation of all the other activities listed. The level of support for prostitution, homosexuality and lesbianism is nevertheless perhaps sufficient for these issues to be too controversial for greater Conservative-Party-inspired repression. However, on surrogate motherhood, firearm possession, ticket touting, narcotics and the sale of human organs there appears to be overwhelming support for State prohibition. In those cases that are currently legal, or partially so, firearm possession and ticket touting, it might even be argued that the leadership of the Conservative Party would become more popular by proposing further legislation against these activities.

Among the youth population one could say that the legalisation of abortion and Sunday trading were consensus issues with over 70 per cent support. Prostitution, surrogate motherhood, homosexuality (male and female) and ticket touting are clearly mainstream activities the legalisation of which would be supported by at least 60 per cent of the youth. Any support by the senior Conservatives for criminalisation would bring the two sides into conflict, with divisions within both groups. Cannabis is remarkably an evenly supported issue, and as such it may be regarded in future surveys as a good indicator as to how the general debate between individual responsibility and social responsibility is going.

Heroin legalisation is supported by 31 per cent of the youth population and opposed by less than two-thirds. This drug, considered extremely addictive, associated with the spread of AIDS via contaminated syringes, and popularly associated with drug overdoses and organised crime, is arguably a candidate for legalisation on grounds of freedom of choice, although there is a body of opinion that considers legalisation desirable for similar reasons as those that prompted the repeal of alcohol prohibition in 1930s America. As such, the figure might come as a shock to those commentators who assumed that heroin legalisation was either the preserve of a tiny 'lunatic fringe' or else associated with the counter-culture rather than the bastions of the establishment.

The figures generally for the youth provide us with a composite stereotype: the Conservative youth of today accepts abortion, prostitution, surrogate motherhood, homosexuality, lesbianism and ticket touting, cannot understand why Sunday trading was not legal until recently, is undecided on cannabis and selling human organs, and objects to firearm possession and heroin consumption.

It is noticeable that these views can best be understood by the notion of 'victimless crime'. The degree to which a victim can be identified as a result of the activities surveyed seems to be the degree to which there is hostility to these activities. The same conclusion may be drawn from the senior population. Apart from homosexuality and lesbianism, the wide gaps between the old and the young can be partly explained by different perceptions of who the victim of the crime is. For the sale of human organs it would appear to be an assumption among the senior population that this is dangerous to the donor and immoral for the recipient. To the young, who have grown up in an age of test-tube babies and genetic engineering, the threat is not perceived in such terms. For firearms, the victim is seen as the innocent bystander caught in the cross-fire of gun-toting maniacs and armed policemen. The spirit of a moral case for individual firearm ownership as a check on State authority is not mainstream Conservative thinking, possibly entirely due to the complacency brought about by relative constitutional stability since 1688. In America, part of the gun lobby issue is that of the right of citizens to overthrow the State if it becomes too oppressive: this is after all what the War of Independence was about. Given the evidence, the Libertarian right's influence from America is clearly not absolute on all the social issues presented.

Turning to the economic issue of privatisation, the Post Office, British Rail and the British Broadcasting Corporation can be said to be operating as commercial enterprises or at least in competition with others. With the privatisation of virtually all the nationalised industries, the deregulation of buses, the sale into the private sector of gas, telecommunications, water and electricity, there is a logical succession which almost invites the privatisation of British Rail, the Post Office and the BBC. Other likely targets include the break-up of London Transport and the sale of remaining government share holdings in private companies like British Telecom. However, the monarchy, the legal system, the higher education system, the police forces, and money are not obviously associated with commercial objectives. The National Health Service is on the agenda only because the opposition parties have persistently claimed for the best part of a decade that it was 'already happening'. The debate is now taking the form of how to make the NHS operate 'like a market', and from some quarters arguments centre on the question 'why not privatise it?'.[9]

Table 5.6 Table of Privatisations

'Do you believe in the privatisation of ... ?'

	Youth				Senior			
	Yes	(%)	No	(%)	Yes	(%)	No	(%)
Post Office	236	83	37	13	66	37	100	57
British Rail	244	86	30	10	82	47	83	47
The Monarchy	83	29	178	63	2	1	162	93
National Health Service	159	56	109	38	28	16	135	77
The Legal System	88	31	173	61	21	12	142	81
The Police Forces	86	30	179	63	6	3	159	91
Higher Education System	162	57	99	35	31	17	134	77
Money	131	46	123	43	11	6	150	86
BBC	208	74	59	20	52	29	113	64

Of the nine privatisations on offer (Table 5.6) none are supported by an overall majority of the senior population. However, five of the nine are favoured by an overall majority of the youth. Within this cleavage there is a consensus as to which are the most desirable and those which are the least. British Rail is the most favoured privatisation in both groups; 47 per cent of seniors favour it, 47 per cent oppose, 86 per cent of young Conservatives favour it, only 10 per cent oppose. Given the fact that government ministers had previously expressed interest in BR privatisation, the opposition to it seems to be the clearest expression of 'wetness' available in the survey. This is worth bearing in mind when examining the composition of the population of anti-Libertarians within the party's youth branches.

The Post Office is the second most favoured privatisation. The order of preference that appears to be taking shape could almost be a referendum on the degree of unpopularity of the various choices on offer. The gap of 46 percentage points between the senior level of support (37 per cent) and the young (83 per cent) is yet more evidence that the virtue of placing enterprises in the private sector is accepted by the young but not by the senior Conservative population.

The unpopularity of the BBC with Conservative Party members has been demonstrated at Conservative Party Conference year after year. Typified by Norman Tebbit's attacks over coverage of the Libyan air raid in 1986, these criticisms have provoked a vengeful desire to break the cosy bureaucracy of State broadcasting. The greater support for privatisation among the young is a reflection on an iconoclastic attitude, with the BBC regarded as an organisation removed from the realities of a market society. The only cure, according to Libertarians, is to remove it from its 'lofty' status as a consumer of public money.

The higher education system and the National Health Service are equally popular as targets for privatisation with yet again a substantial gap (40 percentage points) between youth support and senior support. In both cases the figures are predictable for the senior membership. One in six supports privatisation, almost certainly out of sheer dissatisfaction with the quality of service and in response to scare stories circulated by other political parties. For 77 per cent of the senior membership there is opposition to privatisation, which is clear evidence of the sincerity of Conservative Party claims that there is to be no privatisation of the NHS, whilst higher education privatisation does not even merit a denial.

Among the young the situation is somewhat different. A clear majority of the young surveyed favoured the privatisation of both higher education (57 per cent) and the NHS (56 per cent). The purpose of privatisation was not simply to remove State ownership but also vested interest control through monopoly trade associations. There is a parallel with the ideas of the late nineteenth-century American anarcho-capitalist Benjamin Tucker on the subject of monopoly ownership of capital:[10] the medical profession in America is regulated through a legislatively constructed monopoly – the State Medical Boards. In the UK the analogous organisation is the General Medical Council (GMC). To many young Conservatives, the research of Dr David Green at the Institute of Economic Affairs is known, if not widely read.[11] The conclusions are similar about both the USA and the UK; health problems are to do with restrictive practices of a quasi-closed shop type. Therefore, youth population support for NHS privatisation goes hand in hand with support for the break up of the General Medical Council, with the aim of increasing vastly the range of choice of medical services, and of reducing costs to an affordable level.

Support for privatising money was very high among the young (46 per cent, 3 per cent more than opposed it), but the question appears to have been confusing given an 11 per cent 'no response' and a number of written comments on the questionnaires. Among senior respondents the figures were worse (6 per cent) than for the sale of human organs (7 per cent), suggesting that the question was possibly perceived as an issue of reintroducing barter as opposed to private and competing currencies.

With the legal system and the police the youth population makes little distinction between the amount of support for either as continuing State monopolies, 31 per cent favouring legal system privatisation and 30 per cent police force privatisation. Among senior members the legal system is clearly regarded as a less integral part of the State than the police. There is 10 per cent greater opposition to police privatisation than there is to the privatisation of the legal system. At this stage the figures ought to reflect a cleavage within the party between anarchists and minarchists (or 'minimal-state-anarchists'): legal-system privatisation and possibly police privatisation ought to be substantially less popular with a non-anarchist population. That the figures approximate to 30 per cent could mean that these youth activists are actual anarchists in all but name. If they do not favour State ownership of the legal system or of the police then one must wonder what role there is left for the State. The figures for the privatisation of the Monarchy bear this analysis out.

Indeed, these figures match an internal poll taken by national officers of the Conservative Collegiate Forum in early 1991. When they asked an audience of their branch chairmen and core activists who were 'Anarcho-capitalists', 'Capitalists' or 'Conservatives', it was found that a quarter described themselves as anarchists.[12]

The privatisation of the Monarchy found two supporters amongst a population of 174 senior Party members (1 per cent). Among the youth 29 per cent supported the privatisation of the Monarchy, only 1 per cent fewer than supported the privatisation of the Police and 2 per cent fewer than that of the legal system, clear evidence of a major anarcho-capitalist presence. It is far too simplistic however to believe that this 29 per cent 'hate' or want to 'get rid of' the Monarchy. Many, when questioned, expressed the view that they supported privatisation because they did not want to infringe on the liberties of those individuals who really did not like the Monarchy. They were quite happy to see the Royal Family selling the rights of their weddings to television companies, and earning an income from their estates and royalties on their postcards, but they were opposed to taxpayers' money being used. Many of the young who favour privatisation of the Monarchy, want to be able to pay for it themselves directly. They argue that the market would automatically keep an effective check on the standards of royal behaviour. It would not pay a family member to open a supermarket because it would debase and devalue the institution.[13]

The overall picture of the privatisation debate is one of consistency as to which are the more integral parts of the State and which are the most commercial. There is a gulf between the progressive radicalism of the youth and the reactionary 'immobilist' tendencies of the seniors. The attitude among the senior membership, borne out by the relative acceptance of British Rail privatisation, is that if the Party Leader proposes it then it must be all right, until then it is a 'dangerous and insane' idea. Similar percentages of support would have been found for the privatisation of British Steel, the Water Boards and the electricity industry, before that happened. In some cases they were even more unpopular than the privatisation of the Post Office which is at 57 per cent disapproval and on a par with National Health Service privatisation disapproval at 77 per cent.

The young surveyed could be summed up as supporting Post Office and British Rail privatisation even more than Sunday trading legalisation, overwhelmingly supporting BBC privatisation, and showing a slight overall majority for higher education and NHS privatisation. Money was the most controversial issue with a 3 per cent difference between support and opposition to its denationalisation, but the possible confusion makes it difficult for it to be used as a yardstick of Libertarian penetration. NHS privatisation, being so clearly an issue of commercialising a social service, is probably a better indicator of broadly Libertarian support. By combining the population of cannabis legalisers with NHS privatisers, one should find a Libertarian core population.

The anarcho-capitalists who favour the privatisation of the Monarchy, the police and the legal system are in a minority, yet one of approximately the same standing as the supporters of male homosexual legality among the older members.

The next step in the research was to take the 48 per cent who wanted to see cannabis legalised and deduct from those the respondents who opposed NHS privatisation. The result was 36 per cent of the total youth: close to the lowest percentages recorded among the youth population in favour of any issue. It is this population that can be called the party's Libertarian 'New Wave'. Conversely the opponents of British Rail privatisation could be described as the 'wets'. It would not be advisable to correlate this population with the opponents of one of the legalisations to create a moral and economic opponent of Libertarianism, because by and large it is not possible to predict which issues will be opposed by the wets. In addition to this, the size of the wet population was considered so small, at 30 out of 281, that to reduce it further by introducing additional qualifications would make the margins of error unacceptably high. As it is the margins are such that one different response would change a percentage by 3.5 per cent. It was also found that 6.7 per cent of anti-BR privatisers voted for legalisation of cannabis and privatisation of the NHS.

The notable differences between the New Wave population and the young generally could be found in the universal extent to which they were more inclined to legalise and privatise.

On abortion, the proportions were virtually unchanged, reflecting the different conclusions Libertarians draw on this issue. Firearm possession was now favoured by 60 per cent but heroin overtook firearms and selling human organs as a legitimate area of market activity at 69 per cent. Surrogate motherhood was now supported by 85 per cent and every other activity by 90-100 per cent.

Comparing the New Wave view of privatisation and having taken a population entirely supportive of NHS privatisation the interesting issues were money and the low scoring issues dividing monarchists and anarchists. On money 80 per cent supported, suggesting that the issue was fairly clear to this specific population. Police privatisation was supported by almost two-thirds (61 per cent), that of the Monarchy by 59 per cent, and of the legal system by 54 per cent. The monarchy was not more popular as a state institution than the state-run Judiciary. The majority in favour of legal system privatisation no doubt included the notion of legal reforms as suggested by Lord Mackay, which involved removing some of the restrictive practices operating in the courts. On the form of this survey, this population would want to see more far-reaching changes. The important point to note, however, is that under analysis no privatisation nor legalisation could be found which a majority of the New Wave did not support.

Whilst carrying out the survey, the issue of road pricing became a contentious one and the author has no doubt that, if asked, the New Wave would support it with a substantial majority. Euthanasia and certain forms of experimentation on humans are the only conceivable exceptions to legalisation imaginable, with the armed forces a possible 'controversial' subject for discussion.[14]

Table 5.7 Free Movement

'Do you believe in the international free migration of ... ?'

		Capital		Labour		Property	
		No.	(%)	No.	(%)	No.	(%)
Senior	Yes	146	83	46	26	62	35
	No	18	10	117	67	97	55
Youth	Yes	252	89	185	65	219	77
	No	15	5	83	29	40	14

The only remaining comparison concerned the degree of tolerance for the free migration of labour (Table 5.7). For the established view of the extreme right, namely that it is composed of 'authoritarian nationalists', to be valid, the level of support for the international free migration of labour would have to be lower than that of the Conservative youth as a whole and surely also of the wet population. The actual result indicates that whereas senior support for this issue is 26 per cent and the youth population scored 65 per cent, the young Libertarian New Wave scored 86 per cent compared with the wets at 60 per cent. Without suggesting that the wets conform more easily to the authoritarian paradigm, it must nevertheless be pointed out that the support for the international free migration of labour is 32 per cent above average for Libertarians but 8 per cent below average for the wets. It must also be pointed out that this support among Libertarians was shown in interviews to be for world-wide migration, whereas other groups were often restricted themselves to the European Community.

Therefore, not only are members of the Libertarian New Wave not anti-immigration, they are actually less nationalistic than the rest of their colleagues in the party. Against popular opinion they have an internationalist outlook that is entirely consistent with the view that an ideology has emerged within the Conservative Party that is compatible with the 'globalisation of capitalism'.

Table 5.8 Social Class Distribution

CLASS *	I	II	IIIa	IIIb	IV	V	TOTAL†
Student Population‡ (%)	21	49	11	12	6	1	100
Young Survey Population (%)	19	35	31	8	4	3	100
New Wave Population (%)	23	34	28	10	3	3	101

* Class categories taken from the Registrar General's Classification.
†Figures rounded to nearest whole number.
‡ Student population figures calculated from UCCA Statistical Supplement Table 8.b, in the *1988-9 UCCA Report*.

Table 5.9 Variation of New Wave from
Young Survey Population in terms of Class Background

CLASS *	I	II	IIIa	IIIb	IV	V
New Wave Population (%)	+3	-2	-3	+1	-1	0

* Class categories taken from the Registrar General's Classification.

The quantitative analysis was then made of the class background and religious or secular beliefs of the Libertarian New Wave. The context of the youth population under analysis was that it consisted of predominantly students or former students. The class distribution of the general British student population and of the young survey population in Table 5.8 is broadly similar: the Young Conservatives who have not been students may be the entire cause of the differences in social class IIIa, for instance. Furthermore, the classifications were not made by the same people: UCCA's figures generated the student population breakdown, while the author attributed respondents' occupations and those of their parents to class categories. This introduces a margin of error between the two breakdowns.

The New Wave figures (Table 5.9) are, however, based on precisely the same research as the young survey population with a consequently small margin of error. The New Wave population was 101 out of the total youth population of 281; one alternative response would change a percentage score by no more than 1 per cent including rounding up figures.

It is not possible to attribute any significant class bias to the young Libertarians. There may be some bias within the population as a whole, but nothing with any different significance from that of any other group in the Conservative Party.[15] The Libertarian penetration of the party does not appear – despite the claims of some commentators and the beliefs of many in the party – to be based on the influx of activists from a particular class.

These findings are in contrast to the assessment made by Kelly in his report on the 1986 FCS Conference.[16] Whereas he perceived a class-conscious movement splitting Libertarians from traditional groups, the evidence available contradicts this view. It suggests that the belief of class division is a myth designed to give credibility on both sides. It must be pointed out, however, that there was a 4 1/2 year gap between the Scarborough Conference of April 1986 and the beginning of the survey in October 1990. It may well be that in taking over the Young Conservatives, after the closure of the FCS, the Libertarians were forced to recruit cadres among higher social categories than previously was the case. As a result of the spread of Libertarianism into the YCs it might have been the case that the Libertarians began to be represented at all social levels. Ultimately, this may account for the Libertarian takeover of the Oxford University Conservative Association.

However, if this reconciliation of Kelly's impressions and the survey is accurate then this only goes to compound the misguidedness of the Conservative Party's closure of the FCS. For if the Libertarians of 1986 were originally isolated in a particular class, then as long as they confined their activities to the FCS it is perhaps arguable that they were more easily containable.

CCO appears to have laboured under the delusion that Libertarians either could not or would not spread their ideas into the Young Conservatives, although the initial CCF structures showed some caution in this respect. The notions of anarcho-capitalism and the worldwide struggle against communism were not the reasons why people joined the YCs. There was however a greater politicisation of the YCs largely due to the decline in the social reasons for joining. The greater availability for young people of club entertainment, cinemas, discos etc., detracted from the traditional motives for joining a local YC branch. In the 1980s young people who joined often did so close to election times with the deliberate purpose of supporting the party. Libertarianism, being a new political programme in tune with a radical vision of Thatcherism, was bound to find some supporters who disapproved of the Heathite leadership of the Young Conservatives. This process was speeded up because of the almost public 'war' (mentioned in Chapter IV) between the FCS and the YCs. Therefore, as a consequence of greater availability of Libertarian material and of new politically minded Young Conservative recruits, the class distribution of the New Wave may well have changed over time.

Having examined class and found no current social divergence between being a Libertarian and the rest of the youth population surveyed, the next step is to examine the issues of religiosity and secularity to establish whether or not there is a connection between traditional Conservatives and religion on the one hand, and between Libertarians and atheism or agnosticism on the other. Table 5.10 shows the various percentages of the different groups who responded to an identically worded question. The options available were atheism, agnosticism, Church of England, Church of Scotland, Catholicism, Judaism, Methodism, Islam, and other religions. The total of religious categories was computed on the basis of adding up all but the atheists and the agnostics.

The figures show clear differences between the young and old in the party. This is to be expected given that such differences may be found in the UK population at large.

Table 5.10 Comparative Levels of Religiosity and Secularity

	1	2	3	3i	3ii	3iii	3iv	3v	3vi	3vii
Senior (%)	9	9	78	na	na	na	na	na	na	na
Young (%)	18	20	62	36	4	10	4	4	0	4
New Wave (%)	21	32	48	4	5	5	4	2	0	6
Wets (%)	13	13	73	40	0	13	0	13	0	7

1= Atheist 2=Agnostic 3=Religious Belief Total 3i=Church of England 3ii=Church of Scotland 3iii=Catholic 3iv=Jewish 3v=Methodist 3vi=Muslim 3vii=Other Religions

The clearest gaps are in the levels of atheism and agnosticism between the youth and senior populations. The young are twice as atheistic and agnostic as the seniors. The divergences between the New Wave and the young as well as between the wet population and the young are of similar proportions, but in opposite directions. The wets are close to the senior position as can be ascertained by comparing their position relative to the senior and the youth populations. But the wets were found to represent a mere 10 per cent of the young.

The New Wave is twice as atheistic/agnostic as the wets, and less than two-thirds as likely to belong to the Church of England (the 'Tory Party at prayer'). The figures clearly demonstrate a link between the degree of religiosity or secularity and membership of a particular grouping within the Conservative Party (Appendix I, Section B).

Table 5.11 Correlation between Religion and Ideology
(Percentage of each religious group belonging to
each ideological group)

	1	2	3	3i	3ii	3iii	3iv	3v	3vi	3vii
New Wave	21	32	48	27	4	5	4	2	0	6
(%)	40.4	56.1	27.9	27.0	36.4	17.9	36.4	16.7	0.0	60.0
Wets	4	4	22	12	0	4	0	4	0	2
(%)	7.2	7.0	12.8	12.0	0.0	14.3	0.0	33.3	0	20.0
Total Young	52	57	172	100	11	28	11	12	0	10

1=Atheist 2=Agnostic 3=Religious belief total 3i=Church of England 3ii=Church of Scotland 3iii=Catholic 3iv=Jewish 3v=Methodist 3vi=Muslim 3vii=Other Religions

Table 5.11, which deals with correlations between religion and ideology demonstrates two facts quite clearly, on the subject of agnosticism and Judaism. Because a majority of all agnostics (56 per cent) and over a third of all Jews (36 per cent) are in the New Wave, compared with none in the wets, there is powerful evidence both (a) of relative secularisation and (b) that anti-Semitism cannot be substantiated in connection with membership of the Libertarian right. According to the figures there is more fertile ground for investigating the reasons why none of the Jews surveyed could be associated with the wets.

The Segregation Indices (in Appendix I) show just how far the New Wave is to be distinguished from the survey population as a whole more in its religious or secular outlook than in its class composition. On class the index shows a 5.0 variation, on religiosity there is a 13.7 variation. The other interesting factor is the similar (12.2) variation between the Wets and the survey population. Given the large gap between the New Wave and the Wets on religion and secularism (25.4), there seems to be a correlation between a group of people holding extreme or radical political opinions and that group being composed of a different religious/atheist mixture from those in the centre.

The question: 'Who would you like to see as the next leader of the Conservative Party?' produced 59 different choices – including 'me' as one choice – out of the total youth population of 281 (Full list in Appendix II). The most notable absences were Edward Heath and two right wingers who had previously figured in polls among young Conservatives: John Moore MP and Lord Young. The absence of Ronald Reagan and the presence of George Bush is a reflection of the circumstances of the survey – the early stages of the Gulf crisis in autumn 1990. The three leadership challengers to replace Mrs Thatcher polled approximately in proportion with their actual scores in November 1990. Most of the research was carried out before that date and of the five 'No' replies, four assumed no possibility of change and one response was to the effect 'had already changed'. John Major was clearly ahead of Michael Heseltine, with Douglas Hurd trailing far behind, but Major needed one more vote to secure an overall majority, exactly as in the real poll of MPs. The differences are in the other choices and the sheer dominance of 'sound' candidates.

Norman Tebbit scored three less than John Major and two more than Heseltine. Chris Patten was the only 'left-winger' other than Heseltine to score more votes than Douglas Hurd. Peter Lilley and Mrs Thatcher tied for the same number of clear preferences, (NB, although Mrs Thatcher also had two 'half votes' – where two preferences were given instead of one) and Michael Forsyth, Michael Howard, Michael Portillo, John Redwood and the 'rational self-interested Me' were in a close bunch.

Of the other respondents it is worth noting the non-politicians. Business men are more highly valued by Randian Conservatives than MPs, even those accused of corrupt practices like Asil Nadir of Polly Peck. The philosophers of the New Right are present in this list, but not the ones supposedly admired by them, according to commentators generally. Hayek leads, with more support than Enoch Powell, Geoffrey Howe, and Peter Walker. Murray Rothbard is proposed, Nozick is not. Ayn Rand is proposed – possibly by a respondent who was unaware of her death, but the respondent who asked 'apart from Leonard Peikoff?' not only knew of Rand's death, but presumably also knew that he is the literary executor of her will and that he has set up the Ayn Rand Institute. It would be tempting to assume that when referring to 'Friedman' the respondent who did so meant David and not Milton, the former being an anarcho-capitalist philosopher. Adam Smith was listed, but whether in association with the Scottish philosopher who wrote the *Wealth of Nations* or with the association of thought produced by the Adam Smith Institute, whose President Dr Madsen Pirie got two votes, is not known. What is clear is the total absence of any centre or left Party thinkers. Indeed, the absence of traditional Conservative thinkers such as Burke, Hume, Oakshott and Scruton are a sign that either the wets do not value these people or perhaps more accurately that they do not rate intellectuals at all. The author assumes that the 'Fidel Castro' proposer was a right-wing admirer of guerrilla warfare, a theory supported by the iconography of the right. Che Guevara would have made equal sense.

Arnold Schwarzenegger and 'No One' both in different ways reflect the ideal of the right. The former is the mass killer of Communists in films who has replaced Rambo, the latter can be relied upon not to interfere with the day-to-day activities of the people: the ultimate 'termination' of the State.

A comparison between the leadership choices of the New Wave and the wets separates the slightly confusing results given by the overall poll (see Tables 5.12 and 5.13). Peter Lilley emerges as the clear favourite with Norman Tebbit closely followed by John Major and Chris Patten as the compromise candidates of the extremes. Tebbit's high vote on the 'sound' wing is boosted by votes from the wets, an indication that some elements of radical Thatcherism at any rate hold appeal throughout the youth population. The number of likely contenders on the New Wave side to replace John Major suggests an open field but with a number of choices unthinkable in say 1985. There are four clear choices: Lilley, Redwood, Forsyth and Portillo, who are young, and whose credentials meet the approval of the New Wave in the event of future leadership change. This assumes, of course, that such a change would take place later rather than sooner, in which case Mrs Thatcher's cause might be championed.

On the wets' side, the choice is remarkably small. Leaving aside choices like Waldegrave and Bush who tie, the only clear candidates are Heseltine and Chris Patten. This is in stark contrast with the situation in 1985, when it would have been possible to list multitudes of former wet Cabinet Ministers and up-and-coming wets, compared with Tebbit and usually one 'young pretender' such as John Moore to represent the right.

Table 5.12 New Wave Leadership Poll

Votes *	Name of Candidate
10	Peter Lilley
8	Norman Tebbit
7	John Major – John Redwood
5	Margaret Thatcher
4 1/2	Michael Forsyth
4	Michael Portillo
3 1/2	Teresa Gorman -Me
3	Chris Patten – No one
2 1/2	Michael Heseltine
2	Nicholas Ridley – Tom King – Michael Howard – Tim Janman – Friedrich Hayek
1 1/2	Norman Lamont
1	Enoch Powell – David Mellor – John Knott – Michael Fallon – William Waldegrave – Douglas Hurd – Lord Waddington – Cecil Parkinson – Eric Forth – Francis Maude – William Hague – Fidel Castro – Ayn Rand – Arnold Schwarzenegger – Madsen Pirie – Adam Smith – George Bush – Marc-Henri Glendening
1/2	John Patten – Friedman (David or Milton?) – Murray Rothbard – Leonard Peikoff – Richard Branson – Victor Kiam – Asil Nadir
7	No Replies

* Votes cast in percentages, NB joint preferences = 1/2

Table 5.13 Wet Leadership Poll

Votes Total	Votes %	Name of Candidate
6	20.0	Michael Heseltine – Chris Patten
2	6.7	John Major – Norman Tebbit
1	5.0	Michael Howard – William Waldegrave – Marcus Fox – George Bush – Me – Pro-Europe – It Depends
1/2	1.7	Gillian Shepherd
5	16.7	No Replies

NB joint preferences = 1/2

Overall, the research survey quantifies the cleavage between senior Conservative Party members and the young. However, this latter population was disproportionately student based in the sense that a large number of respondents were recent or current students. This made an evaluation of educational background unrepresentative and therefore of little value to the research. Similarly, the class background was affected and the small representation of certain classes led to large margins of error in the study of class/ideology correlations. The overall religious beliefs and secularism tallies were sufficient to ensure generally more acceptable degrees of statistical precision. The correlation between class and a particular ideology was insufficient to distinguish it from margins of error. The correlation between religion or secular belief and a particular ideology was pronounced far beyond margins of error and showed opposite belief systems tending towards opposite political views. However, it is not possible to ascertain which was cause and which was effect.

The old population in the Conservative Party during 1990-1 could be generalised as religious, in favour of free movement of capital but nothing or no one else, slightly favouring legal abortions and Sunday trading, undecided on British Rail privatisation, and hostile to all the other legalisations and privatisations proposed.

The average young Conservative is probably religious but favours the free migration of all goods, capital, and labour. He/she favours legal abortion, prostitution, surrogate motherhood, homosexuality (male and female), Sunday trading, ticket touting, is undecided on cannabis and the selling of human organs, but opposes firearm possession and heroin. He/she is a minimal statist wanting to keep only the monarchy, the legal system and the police forces under State ownership, and is not quite sure about private currencies.

The Wets, those who oppose British Rail privatisation, are almost indistinguishable from their seniors in terms of religious belief, the difference being that they are not the mainstream of their generation. On free migration they are less keen, even though many of them only consider free migration in terms of Europe rather than the world. They have two clear leaders, Michael Heseltine and Chris Patten, but do not rate Edward Heath highly.

The New Wave representative is a latent anarcho-capitalist. He/she overwhelmingly favours all legalisations with a slight preference for firearm possession, heroin legalisation, and the selling of human organs. He/she thinks 'everything ownable should be privately owned': Monarchy, the NHS, the legal system, police forces, and currencies. Importantly, the New Wave is not religious, and is more likely to be agnostic than Church of England, with a strong atheist streak. He/she has a long list of possible future leaders and regards philosophers, economists, or himself/herself as a worthy alternative to the politician in charge.

This last group, the Libertarian New Wave, is the radical wing of the party's youth. It defies conventional demonologies of those who see racist, jack-booted illiterates as the extreme opposite to Social-ism. It puts the traditional spectrum of political ideology on a new axis, between individualism and collectivism, both within the party and in the field of social and political science generally.

5.3 Putting the Record Straight

To date, most analyses of the Conservative Party's Libertarians have framed them as authoritarian extremists. Frequently, views have been attributed to the Libertarians that do not fit with the research findings of this study and as such fail to explain their nature in a rig-orous manner. It can be argued that journalists, academics and many politicians have systematically misrepresented this new generation. Perhaps at a loss to describe them, commentators have fallen into the trap of employing out-dated explanations. Nowhere can this mistake be more clearly identified than with regard to the FCS's perceived attitude to South Africa and apartheid. For the view was persistently conveyed that FCS extremism was tied up with an admiration of South African racism. Whilst proclaiming the Libertarians' advoca-tion of free-market values commentators rarely followed the argu-ments through to their logical conclusion. For example, while reports frequently spoke in the following terms:

> After its critical report on extreme Right Wing infiltration into the Party there is still a feeling that the Tory leadership and hierarchy is compla-cent about the entryist threat.
> Recent FCS forays into Northern Ireland – opposing the Anglo-Irish Agreement – and into South Africa – supporting apartheid – are regarded by many as extremist activity which should not be tolerated.[17]

No attempt was made to explain how these extremists supposedly reconciled their anarchic views with the authoritarian powers of the South African state. Locked into an out-dated perspective of what it means to be a right-wing extremist, commentators have often been left to attribute a contradictory and incoherent set of views which do not add up. To cover the gaps journalists in particular have produced eclectic and illogical theories which do not fit together.

Contrary to popular opinion, the FCS viewed racism as another form of 'state imposed collectivism' and was opposed to it on principle. Hence, at the 1986 FCS conference, motion No. 1 amendment No. 2 read:

> Conference believes:
> 1)That the reforms should be welcomed and that the South African Government should be encouraged further to dismantle the system of ethnic socialism called Apartheid.
> 2) That support for the ANC which is ideologically in sympathy with, and receives assistance from the Soviet Union is profoundly unconservative.
> 3) That disinvestment, as Chief Buthelezi, has emphasised, would only serve to exacerbate the difficulties faced by South African blacks and should be vigorously resisted.
> 4) That the free enterprise, capitalist system, if allowed to operate, can and will emancipate blacks as it is colour blind and responds to market forces, not racial prejudices.[18]

Away from the traditional politics of authoritarianism and imperialism the FCS argued against apartheid. They wanted to break the South African system through the free market. By trading with and investing in South Africa they believed capitalism could undermine the state's control and force change.[19]

Far from having the slightest sympathy with racism or apartheid the libertarians possessed a systematic and sophisticated analysis of both. Chris Tame's Bibliography of Freedom, published by the Centre for Policy Studies in 1980, and highly influential amongst Young Conservative Radicals, contained sections on the economics of racism and the libertarian critique of racism enunciated by Ayn Rand and Jacques Barzun. Rand characterised racism as 'the lowest form of collectivism' in an influential essay 'Racism' in her *The Virtue of Selfishness: A New Concept of Egoism.*

Free market economists, including black libertarians like Thomas Sowell and Walter Williams, also developed a detailed analysis of the origins of racism in state interventionism, and saw the free market (and not anti- or positive-discrimination legislation) as the only effective means for undermining such economic irrationality.[20]

The Libertarian view on drugs, like those on South Africa, has also been frequently misrepresented. When in 1984 FCS Chairman Marc-Henri Glendening was reported as supporting heroin legalisation, the issue was popularly perceived in crude terms of the FCS advocating drug usage. A permissive package was attached to the ideology that detracted from its core argument based upon supply side economics. Libertarians advocate legalisation because they believe decriminalisation would actually discourage use. For the Libertarian writer Paul

Anderton there are several reasons why state penalties for possession and supply of drugs make the situation worse.[21] Anderton argues that the increased risks involved in the criminalised drugs market implies larger profits for the successful entrepreneur. The profits in turn attract more traders hoping also to make big money, which in turn increases the supply of the goods in demand. For Libertarians the 'problem' gets worse from the supply side because repressive measures in fact encourage an increase in supply. The high prices induced by State restrictions and repression force the less prosperous users to finance their habits by selling supplies to others. These supplies are usually adulterated – or 'cut' – and it is the substances used for adulteration that really cause the diseases so often attributed to the drugs themselves. For many Libertarians, the tragedy of making drugs illegal is that children are seen as an easy market and the habit is spread down the age range. Contrary to public perceptions, Libertarians see drug legalisation as a practical and worthy response to the drugs problem; the FCS never condoned their use.

Given such clear opinions it is perhaps surprising that commentators have so frequently failed to present the Libertarian case properly on such issues as drugs and South Africa. However, given the intergenerational nature of paradigm-shifts in general, it is perhaps understandable that such a revolutionary world-view has taken so long to be recognised.

5.4 Libertarianism as Baby Boom Politics

It is notable that a number of researchers in America have recently argued that the post-war baby boom generation has broken the traditional left-right, Liberal-Conservative dichotomy. They have suggested that there is something so fundamentally different about the children of the 1950s and 1960s that they make nonsense of the old left/right spectrum. In line with the findings of this study, Maddox and Lilie argue that political scientists, pollsters and journalists have traditionally divided voters into the Liberal (in the American sense) and Conservative camps on the basis of two questions that are today inadequate: whether to expand or decrease government intervention in the economy, and whether to expand or decrease civil liberties or personal freedoms. A person who supported government activism and a strong case defence of civil liberties was a 'Liberal'. Someone who opposed economic intervention as well as the expansion of personal freedom was a 'Conservative'.

Away from this traditional view Maddox and Lilie argue that the answers to these questions may be combined to form a total of four, not two, positions. Thus, a person might support economic intervention but oppose the expansion of personal freedoms, or he might oppose economic intervention while supporting personal freedoms. While standard political analysis defines these people as 'inconsistent', Maddox and Lilie describe them as 'populists' and 'Libertarians', and they have demonstrated that in America today there are just as many voters in these two camps as in the two traditional categories.[22]

Markus and Jennings of the University of Michigan, in their on-going study of the high-school class of 1965, find a fiscally conservative/socially liberal strain among the 'Yuppie' element of the baby boomers. Defining the Yuppies as those individuals with a college degree, a professional or managerial job, and a family income of $30,000 or more – some 15 per cent of the group – Markus and Jennings found that in 1973 the (future) Yuppies in the class were more Liberal than their classmates, but that by 1982 they had become markedly more Conservative on economic issues.[23] In 1982 the major political differences among the generation revolved around social issues, with the Yuppies being more Liberal.

However, while many commentators, like Markus and Jennings, attribute the economic Conservatism of the Yuppies to their high incomes, David Boaz has argued:

> It would seem, however, that the years from 1965 to 1982 offered ample opportunity for intellectual and practical disillusionment with government economic programmes. Also the best educated generation in American history surely was influenced to some extent by the important critiques of macroeconomic planning, regulation, and the Welfare State offered by such people as F. A. Hayek, Milton Friedman, Thomas Sowell, George Gilder, and Charles Murray.[24]

Boaz argues that one explanation for the rise of this generation in America is that the baby boomers shared some important experiences and perceptions that set them apart from their elders. When their parents were growing up, government was the institution that ended the Depression and won the Second World War. In the baby-boomer's lives government fought a very unpopular war, a President resigned in disgrace, and government economic planning led to inflation, unemployment and stagflation. For many young Americans government did not solve problems, it created them.

Boaz suggests that, unlike their parents, members of the younger generation have had enough education to be comfortable questioning the decisions of political leaders. He argues that this sceptical attitude first came to the fore in the 1960s when people began to march for Civil Rights and then against the war in Vietnam. He argues that a cultural revolution took place, first on campuses and then generally throughout the West, as young people began to question many of the rules that had seemed certain to their parents. While in America it has become a cliché to say that the baby boomers are fiscally Conservative and socially Liberal, clichés nevertheless are often founded on truth. Many polls show that this generation is more Conservative on economic issues than older voters, but that they retain the social Liberalism – and 'tolerance' – acquired during the 1960s and after.

D. Quinn Mills, a Harvard Business School professor and the author of a book on baby boom executives, *The New Competitors*, estimates that 60 per cent of young American managers could be considered Libertarian.[25] Similarly, an analysis studying young corporate executives in the United States concluded: '... Baby boom business leaders are taking a fresh look at politics. Neither consistent Liberals or Conservatives, they oppose Government intervention in both the economy and their personal lives.'[26]

Although American social and political history is of course different in many respects to that of Britain there are nevertheless important similarities. In many ways the young Libertarians central to this study can be understood in the context of a somewhat similar recent history to that of the US, a history that is, however, so recent, and a generation so new, that they have not yet entered popular consciousness. As David Boaz states:

> Pollsters, journalists and political practitioners seem to have an uncontrollable urge to put every politician and thinker into the Liberal box or the Conservative box. Increasingly, though, these terms fail to describe many Americans, and our understanding of politics has not caught up with reality.[27]

Just as American 'pollsters, journalists and political practitioners' have not yet 'caught up with reality', so it can be argued many in Britain have not yet caught up with the reality of those in the Conservative Party's youth wings – and its products of the 1960s and 1970s.

Notes and References

1. It tends to be only active members who go on to remain involved in party politics in the long term. It is estimated that nearly 40 per cent of all Conservative MPs have been members of the Young Conservatives at some point in their political careers.

2. Although the Conservative Associations surveyed wish to remain anonymous, three were in London, one in the West Country, one in Scotland and one in the North Western area.
3. Schuman, H., and Presser, S., (1981) *Questions and Answers in Attitude Surveys*, New York, Academic Press.
4. This list included those key free market, authoritarian, and socialist politicians most frequently mentioned by Conservative Party Libertarian activists when in conversation with the author.
5. Thomas, R., (1991) *The Nature of Nazi Ideology*, Historical Notes, No. 15, London, Libertarian Alliance.
6. See: Kirkpatrick, J., (1982) *Dictatorships and Double Standards*, New York, Simon and Schuster.
7. For a Libertarian perspective on the international free migration of labour see: Chacksfield, A., (1991) *Open The Door! The Case for Abolishing All Immigration Controls*, Political Notes No. 61, London, Libertarian Alliance.
8. Since the 1970s, public houses in Scotland have been able to remain open from 11 a.m. until 12 p.m. England and Wales followed in 1988. Some Young Conservatives had campaigned on this issue since the early 1980s. See: Moulin, M., (1985/6) *Blueprint*, Greater London Young Conservatives.
9. Arguing for the total privatisation and de-regulation of medicine see: Micklethwait, B., (1991) *How and How Not to Demonopolise Medicine*, Political Notes No. 56., London, Libertarian Alliance.
10. See: Tucker in Woodcock, G., (1977) *The Anarchist Reader*, Hassocks, Sussex, The Harvester Press, pp. 145–8.
11. See, for example, Green, D., (1985) *Working Class Patients and the Medical Establishment*, Hownslow, Temple Smith.
12. The meeting, a CCF training weekend, was held in Nottingham in mid-April 1991. It was attended by around fifty key Conservative Student activists and branch chairmen from around the country.
13. Clarke, A., (1991) *The Precarious Influence of British Royalty*, Historical Notes No. 14, London, Libertarian Alliance.
14. See: Micklethwait, B., (1987) *Taking Free Market Defence Seriously*, Foreign Policy Perspectives No. 7, London, Libertarian Alliance. Micklethwait, B., (1983) *In Praise of Mercenaries*, Political Notes No. 11, London, Libertarian Alliance.
15. The Segregation Index for the New Wave to the Conservative Youth Population is 5, whereas the S.I. compared with the British Student Population is 20.5 and 21.5 respectively (see Appendix I, Section A). Clearly the New Wave does not represent the implantation of a new class of Young Conservative; the New Wave's class background is as typical as that of his ideological competitors within the Conservative Youth Population.
16. Kelly, R., (1989) *Conservative Party Conferences: The Hidden System*, Manchester, Manchester University Press, pp. 109, 114–15.
17. *Guardian*, 8 February 1986, p. 2.
18. See: *FCS Conference Motions: Scarborough*, 1986.
19. Rand, A., (1964) *The Virtue of Selfishness*, New York, New American Library. See also Tame, C. R., 'Racism as the Lowest Form of Collectivism: On The Ideological Nature of Racism', Libertarian Alliance Conference, 'Racism and Anti-Racism: Liberal Perspectives', London, 25 August, 1990. Rand's views were also developed by the black sociologist Anne Wortham in her *The Other Side of Racism*, Ohio State University Press, 1981; 'Equal Opportunity versus Individual Opportunity', *The Freeman*, July 1975, 25(7), pp. 416–23; 'Individuality and Intellectual Independence', *The Freeman*, August 1975, 25(8), pp. 463–71; 'Response to "The Rape of the Black Mind"', *Reason*, 1975, 7(5), pp. 20–7; 'A Black Writer's View of "Roots"', *Libertarian Forum*, March 1977, X(3), pp. 5–6; 'An Open Letter to Nathan Glazer', *Reason*, 1977, 9(5), pp. 25–7; 'A Decision Against Meritorious Achievement', *The Freeman*, August 1978, 28(10), pp. 611–16.

20. See, for example: Sowell, T., (1972) *Black Education: Myths and Tragedy*, New York, David McKay; (1984) *Civil Rights: Rhetoric or Reality*, New York, William Morrow; (1987) *Compassion Versus Guilt*, New York, William Morrow; (1981) *Race and Economics, Minorities*, Oxford, Basil Blackwell; (1984) *Is Reality Optional?, and Other Essays*, New York, Hoover Institution Press; (ed.), (1980) *American Ethnic Groups*, Washington DC, The Urban Institute; (1982) *The State Against Blacks*, New York, McGraw Hill; (1977) 'Government Sanctioned Restraints That Reduce Economic Opportunities for Minorities', *Policy Review*, No. 2, pp. 7–30; (1979) 'Racism and Organised Labour', *Lincoln Review*, 1(1), pp. 25–33.

On the black libertarians, see Conti, J. G. and Stetson, B., (1993) *Challenging the Civil Rights Establishment: Profiles of a New Black Vanguard*, Westport, Conn., Praeger Books.

Other major contributions include: Becker, G., (1971) *The Economics of Discrimination*, 2nd edn, Chicago, University of Chicago Press; Coats, W. L., (1974), 'The Economics of Discrimination', *Modern Age*, 18(1), pp. 64–70; Rabushka, Alvin, (1974) *A Theory of Racial Harmony*, University of South Carolina Press.

On South Africa, see Horwitz, R., (1967) *The Political Economy of South Africa*, London, Weidenfeld and Nicolson; Hutt, W. H., (1964) *The Economics of the Colour Bar*, London, André Deutsch and Institute of Economic Affairs; Hutt, W. H., (1975) South Africa's Salvation in Classical Liberalism, in Pejovich, S., and Klingman, D., (eds) *Individual Freedom: Selected Works of W. H. Hutt*, Westport, Connecticut, Greenwood Press; Wassenarr, A. D., (1977) *Assault on Private Enterprise*, Cape Town, Tafelberg Publishers; Williams, W. E., (1989) *South Africa's War Against Capitalism*, Westport, Conn., Praeger; Lewis, R. et al., (1986) *Apartheid – Capitalism or Socialism?*, London, Institute of Economic Affairs.

21. Anderton, P., (1986) *Drug Abuse: Appearance, Reality and Treatment*, Political Notes, No. 2., London, Libertarian Alliance.

22. Maddox, W. S., and Lilie, S. A., (1989) *Beyond Liberal and Conservative: Reassessing the Political Spectrum*, Washington DC, CATO Institute.

23. See: Boaz, D., (ed.) (1987) *Left, Right and Babyboom*, Washington DC, CATO Institute, pp. 3–4.

24. Ibid., p. 4.

25. Ibid.

26. Ibid.

27. Maddox, W. S. and Lilie, S. A., *Beyond Liberal and Conservative*, p. vii.

CONCLUSION

Maggie's Militants:
A Sociology of Conservative Party Libertarian Youth

....

6.1   The Libertarians: Britain's First Post-Modern Political Youth Movement

Before the rise of the Conservative Party's Libertarians, Abrams and Little concluded there was little evidence to suggest the emergence of a new political generation within British youth politics.[1] They argued that the youth activists of all parties were constrained to work in old institutions and accept old possibilities. The majority of activists during the mid-1960s were merely continuing family traditions of engagement in public affairs, which had often begun as a consequence of key 'politicising experiences' three generations away. The Dock Strike, the Revolution of 1905, and the Great War were all cited as important events that had brought many into politics.

For a majority in the FCS, however, such a family tradition did not exist. In contrast to their predecessors, not only did many of their parents vote for another party, but a substantial majority came from politically inactive backgrounds with no tradition of party membership.[2] For these activists, the devaluation of the pound in 1967, the IMF loan of 1976 and the 1978–9 winter of discontent were the critical activating experiences.[3] The 'stagflation' and legitimation crisis characteristic of the 1970s persuaded many to enter politics for the first time. As one typical ex-FCS member put it:

Notes for this section begin on page 138.

> I was sick of the power cuts in the 70s and the trade unions. I was sick of everybody trying to make socialism work. When the winter of discontent came and then Thatcher was elected I decided to join the FCS. For years I had been a left-wing anarchist but thought that the Conservatives with their privatisation could overthrow the state long before the Labour Party would.[4]

As the product of 'crisis' the Libertarians can be seen to represent historically not only a break with the past in terms of family activism but more importantly a break with accepted political ideology. As Antonio Gramsci argued, under the conditions of a general or 'organic crisis', as seen in the 1970s, new ideologies and social formations emerge.[5]

Since the mid-1980s an array of books, articles and academic papers have argued that western society is on the verge of entering, or has already entered, a new era. Under such headings as 'new times', 'post-fordism' and 'disorganised capitalism',[6] a new agenda of individualism, commercialism, cultural relativism and globalisation has been widely discussed and promoted by authors generally associated with the intellectual left. Yet the post-modernist agenda echoes precisely those ideas and values that have been developed and articulated by the young Libertarian right over the last twenty years. Their advocation of the international free migration of capital, property and labour shares many of the anti-statist impulses characteristic in post-modernist thought.

In a paper entitled *Towards a Post-Modernist Conservatism,* ex-FCS chairman Marc-Henri Glendening examined the rise of the young Libertarian right in the context of recent social development. For him, these activists are best understood as the cultural product of an increasingly integrated world that is itself demanding the transcendence of the traditional nation state. Looking at post-modernist youth culture in general, Glendening stated:

> Access to different ways of seeking cultural self-fulfilment has been facilitated by post-fordist production, mass communications, improved travel facilities and the collapse of residential 'apartheid'. These factors have helped to produce a proliferation of 'style tribes' which evolve, dissolve and fuse with other cultural segments. Individuals now enjoy the means to change cultural identity far more easily than their parents. The organic communities of pre-industrial and fordist Britain which were largely the result of circumstance (where you were born, where you worked) are being replaced in the big cities by a multiplicity of 'designer' communities composed of individuals who share similar attitudes and lifestyles, and seek each other out on that basis.[7]

For Glendening, this fragmentation of once monolithic social blocks into small sub-cultures is one of the key features of contemporary social life. The incorporation of cultural diversity can be seen in many areas, not least architecture, art and popular music. Bhangra, for example, as a mélange of traditional Indian folk music and western rock, is a typical post-modernist phenomena.

Expressions of such thought are not hard to come by in contemporary Conservative youth structures. In 1991 CCF drafted a document entitled *New Times: Post-Thatcherism in the 1990s*. Opposed to monolithic social blocks and extolling the virtues of cultural diversity, it stated:

> We look for a world where individuals' different goals and values are reconciled through the spontaneous order of individual relations rather than the intolerant politicisation of the private lives of the people that socialists and fascists see as the ideal state of society.
>
> We look for a world of staggering diversity where each person can go out and shape their own lives as they wish and exploit a rich array of opportunities …
>
> We want to throw off the dead hand of the socialist, corporatist state and give the people the chance to build the society they desire; where there is wealth enough to feed the hungry and heal the sick, to educate our children and then pass it on to them. This can only be if we let the creative power of individuals express itself in the market, for which we have to set them free.[8]

Unlike the Young Conservatives of the early 1960s and their forebears, the Libertarian right reject the diffuse patriotic politics of traditional Conservatism. They have little feeling for the nation, the monarchy and the established order of society. They are post-modern radicals with a world-view that attempts to cut across boundaries of geography and ethnicity, class and nationality, religion and ideology.

Yet for all their cultural relativism they are also moral absolutists in that they do not deny the existence of 'good' and 'bad'. For them a 'moral' society allows individuals to choose their own lifestyle freely. Providing other's property rights are not violated, it lets them 'do their own thing'. If an individual or a group wants to establish a socialist community then they are free to do so, providing it is organised and paid for only by those who wish to participate and it is undertaken on private property. Freedom does not mean that individuals can impose their will on others.

The Japanese writer Kenichi Ohmae argues that monolithic political and religious beliefs are being undermined by the power and technology of a progressively integrated and advanced world. Uniform and absolutist belief systems are being eroded as cultures are forced to relativise and mix. Analysing the psychological impact of post-modernist culture on the West's young, Ohmae asserts that as

the sociological products of television, the Boeing 747, satellite com-
munications and personal computers, the young of today perceive
the state and the preservation of national cultural identity to be
somewhat unsophisticated and anachronistic objectives. Instead,
they espouse the political virtues of individualism, social toleration
and the culture of 'one-worldism':

> My observations over the past decade seem to indicate that the young
> people of the advanced countries are becoming increasingly nationality-
> less and more like 'Californians' all over the Triad countries – The United
> States, Europe, and Japan – that form the Interlinked Economy.[9]

6.2   The 'Californianisation' of Conservative Youth Structures

According to Chris Tame, Director and founder of the Libertarian
Alliance, Libertarians are philosophically '... vehement and extreme
rationalists'. Following the conclusions regarding secularism in
Chapter V, he argues: 'Almost to a man and a woman they are atheists, they pride themselves in applying rational thought to every
aspect of life and the universe.'[10]

To many Libertarians, the potential for human rationality knows
no bounds. Hence many are involved in that most Californian of
post-modernist pursuits, the life extension and cryonics movement.[11]
However, this is understandable since both cryonicists and Libertarians tend to associate religion with ignorance and irrationality. As
one free market activist put it, modern industrial life means that:

> The gods have deserted us and our clever excuses for oblivion are wear-
> ing thin. In our hearts we know that there is something very wrong with
> our condition, and yet faced with the seeming inevitability of our fate we
> recoil from the obvious implications: we must save ourselves or perish.
>
> Denied the prospect of survival through supernatural agency secular
> Western man has become psychically traumatised. Increasingly life
> seems meaningless and absurd, and the fear of death and nothingness lie
> just below the surface of every day consciousness. Although the struc-
> tures and institutions of religious belief linger, their function is now
> largely sentimental and ceremonial. The once faithful have deserted to
> the post-psychedelic spiritual supermarket in a frantic search for new
> answers to the problem of death.[12]

The British Libertarian David Nicholas argues that the 'continuing fact of death renders all talk of Liberty ultimately futile'.[13] For
him, the popular notion of freedom that passively accepts the cer-
tainty of 'personal extinction' is anti-ego and anti-man. As for many

other Libertarians, death is perceived in terms of being a problem to be scientifically overcome:

> Fortunately a small but growing band of heretics – fringe scientists and speculative writers – are challenging the current paradigm, and providing a platform for a legitimate discussion of the field. They argue with increasing confidence that science and technology can deliver what religion once promised; the age-old dream of immortality may not have been wrong but they depended more on faith than fact. Scientific progress has now begun to allow personal immortality at least to be brought within the bounds of practical speculation.[14]

In her book, *Cryonics: A Sociology of Death and Bereavement*, Arlene Sheskin views the cryonics movement in terms of being the natural, inevitable product of industrial society. Cryonicists are a psychological manifestation of Weberian disenchantment:

> … the cryonic attempt to apply the powers of science to death seems to have been inevitable, given the emphasis on science as a means of salvation in industrial societies. So while cryonicists by associating religion with irrationality and ignorance and invoking science to death seem to have been inevitable given the emphasis on science as a means of understanding and conquering death – a topic previously thought unfathomable to the lay person – the disenchantment of the world of which Weber spoke seems complete.[15]

A disproportionately high number of Libertarians have an interest in science fiction.[16] Like cryonics, this genre embodies strong Faustian or Promethean impulses. The spirit of individualism, of self-confident rationality, of bold conjecture and refutation, the assumption of the accessibility of reality to human intelligence and the possibility and desirability of enhancing human existence are all strong features. For many Libertarians, science fiction is an important past-time because, in the words of Robert A. Heinlein, it 'preaches the need for freedom of the mind and the desirability of knowledge; it teaches that prizes go to those who study, who learn, who soak up the difficult fields such as mathematics and engineering and biology.'[17]

According to Chris Tame in his paper, *Life, Liberty and the Stars: The Ideological Significance of Science Fiction*, science fiction sprang from 'the progressive beliefs that are the essence of science', and that the 'spirit of science is the spirit of enterprise'.[18] Science fiction's reliance upon a voluntaristic and rationalistic image of man parallels the Libertarian view. For many Libertarians, science fiction provides a rational opposition to alienation:

> I am not a stranger and I am not afraid in a world I am happy to make … I am damned from here to eternity only if I abandon my human intel-

ligence and, sheepishly, give up the struggle! That is the answer of science fiction, and that is why it is alive ... [19]

For literary critic P. Schuyler Miller a contrast can be made between the collectivist view of man in mainstream literature and the individualistic stance implicit within classical science fiction:

> In the present mode of mainstream fiction (Everyman) is a symbol for a humanity to whom the world – society, the system, the Establishment – does things. He may struggle; he may fight back; he will certainly scream and make speeches; but he is essentially passive – a born loser.
>
> The Everyman of science fiction, on the contrary, does things to the world. He is the subject, not the object of the action. He schemes, he fights, and he may talk too much, but he assumes that he can and will win ... and usually does. [20]

The theme of the rational, competitive and triumphant ego is central to the ethos of the Libertarian movement. Individualism, enterprise and science are fused into a powerful neo-religious synthesis that replaces god and the collectivity with man and the open society. As David Nicholas argued in his psychologically illuminating paper *Immortality: Liberty's Final Frontier.* 'It will be science, intellect and analysis that will be our salvation – not mysticism ... . We can only engineer our freedom from death not pray for it ... having invented the gods we can turn into them. [21]

Another movement attempting to 'engineer its freedom from death' goes under the name of the Extropians. Led in Britain by the American anarcho-capitalist Russell E. Whitaker, extropians believe it will soon be possible to copy the entire contents of the human mind onto something like a computer's hard disk and thus live forever. According to them, technology will soon enable the creation of computer replicas that in turn will allow humans to leave their bodies yet remain alive electronically.

The Second Law of Thermodynamics states that all differentials in energy level between bodies will eventually be levelled out. Hot things will become colder and cold things will become hotter, until the universe becomes a homogeneous mix of molecules with no concentration of energy at all. Physicists call this state 'entropy': the inexorable tendency of everything to move towards disorder and decay.

In opposition to this law, a number of Los Angeles scientists and academics have coined the term 'Extropy', and established an Extropy Institute. Its magazine, *Extropy – The Journal of Transhumanist Thought*, is edited by the Libertarian philosopher and academic Max More. Iterating the movement's basic principles: (1) boundless expansion; (2) transformation; (3) dynamic optimism, and (4) cooperative diversity, the publication disseminates new, innovative and challenging ideas. It concentrates on what it calls the philosophy of transhumanism, which:

> ... seeks the continuation and acceleration of the evolution of intelligent life beyond its currently human form and human limitations by means of science and technology, guided by progressive principles and values, while rejecting dogma and religion.[22]

Significantly, both More and Whitaker claim to have been proto-Extropians since they were children. At the age of ten, More started to consume vitamin C tablets to extend his life, while Whitaker claims to have been profoundly affected by the science fiction of Robert Heinlein.

According to David Gale, who has investigated the extropian movement extensively, a closer reading of their material uncovers a strong political dimension. Commenting on More and Whitaker he notes:

> In article after article, More inveighs against the interventionism of the welfare state, the doom-mongering ecologists who would impede technological development and the die-hard Marxist demagogues who yearn to fetter the free market.
>
> Whitaker is perfectly explicit about the Extropian's rightish thing. 'Most Extropians start out with an interest in computers and science fiction, but politically we are anarcho-capitalist.'
>
> 'We tend to be libertarians, what some people would consider to be of an extreme persuasion, but we consider ourselves fairly reasonable.'[23]

Summing up the psychological spirit of the whole Libertarian movement, with all its sub-groups, Chris Tame has argued, Libertarians:

> ... don't see the universe as a hostile place, they see [it] as the playground for evolving man to manifest himself in, to control, and ... to seek his happiness in every area.... . Death and taxes is what we want to abolish.... . Most Libertarians are ideological immortalists, we are not content merely with four score years and ten for Christ's sake. We want the universe and we want immortality.[24]

The Libertarian themes of vehement rationalism and radical individualism clearly dominate many minds in the youth wings of the post-Thatcherite Conservative Party. Writing recently in *The Times*, for example, Bryan Appleyard noted:

> ... occasionally there are things one does of such rare, intense folly that they stand out from the usual wash of regrettable phenomena. This one involves the Conservative party ...
>
> At the weekend I took part in a debate about religion, morality and the state with a group known as Conservative Graduates.
>
> ... Their ruthless views echo the Trotskyism and Maoism that gripped students in the Sixties and Seventies.

... Any mention of God brought jeers of dissent.... . the audience was
clearly too bigoted and cruelly lacking in self-doubt for the idea of morality to be remotely convincing.[25]

6.3   Post-Modernity's Comrades:
Ideology and Power in the Conservative Party

According to many commentators,[26] including Abrams and Little,
the parliamentary leadership of the Conservative Party are a dominant group who ruthlessly control the party's agenda and allow little
that can be construed as representing internal party debate and
democracy. The annual conference's stage-managed nature is often
read as being indicative of the party establishment's ability directly
to control and repress local association opinion and ideas.[27]

It was Robert Michels who began his 1911 work, *Political Parties*,
with the observation that as party organisations develop they
inevitably appoint full-time officials and professional politicians who
by their bureaucratic nature erode democracy.[28] For Michels, the
administrative tasks involved in party organisation automatically
lead to the creation of a bureaucratic structure that is anti-democratic. As a party grows, so a division of labour is required that progressively necessitates control and coordination from the top. Thus
all political parties end up largely excluding their members from the
participation and decision making processes; control by a small élite
conforms to the 'iron law of oligarchy'.

Yet, for all the supposed iron control and authority of the Conservative Party's leadership, a new political youth movement has
been allowed to emerge in recent years which in challenging the
views of the party's elders undermines Michels' theory. The Libertarians, with their anarchic anti-statism, idealistic internationalism
and ungodly rationalism, represent the survival and perpetuation of
internal oppositional thought. Ultimately they represent the antithesis of traditional Burkeian Conservatism. For while Burke adhered to
the authority of religion, prescription, instinct and communitarianism, the Libertarians place their faith in the authority of reality, reason, man and capitalism.

Examining the party's accommodation of the Libertarians, Brian
Micklethwait, of the Libertarian Alliance, argues that ultimately
British Conservatism has no fixed philosophy, no concrete ideolog-
ical base, other than the attempt at humane and successful govern-
ment by whatever seems appropriate at any given time.[29] Unlike the
Labour Party with 'Clause IV',[30] the Conservatives are an inherently

fluid political organisation with no fixed policies. Micklethwait
argues that the closure of the FCS was therefore not about the party's
objection to Libertarianism but its unease at the FCS's style of
activism. Paramilitary excursions to the third world, widespread
vote-rigging and the FCS's image of violence were what concerned
the party. For him, hard-core Libertarianism is allowed to thrive in
its post-FCS youth wings because its proponents are more measured
in their appearance and approach: 'Providing they are wearing shirts
and ties and not shouting too loudly they are free to believe in whatever they want, including anarchy.'[31]

6.4 Libertarianism as Paradigm-Shift

The traditional distinction between Conservatism and ideational ideologies has led some non-Conservatives to deny any intellectual con-
tent to Conservatism and has led some Conservatives to attack all
ideologies. However, for Samuel P. Huntington both the critics and
defenders of Conservatism are wrong. For him Conservatism is ultimately '… the rational defence of being against mind, of order
against chaos'.[32] It is about '… articulate, systematic, theoretical resistance to change'.[33] Huntington's view of Conservative politics is
popular. Yet, like Michels's theory, it fails to explain the emergence
and survival of a radical school of thought within the party that is
ultimately opposed to such principles. It fails to explain the emergence of a school whose epistemology is reason, ethics-self-interest
and politics-anarcho-capitalist.

While in the mid-1960s Abrams and Little concluded that the
Young Conservatives were 'thoroughly at one'[34] with their elders,
and asserted: 'There is no new generation so far as the Conservative
Party is concerned',[35] the inexorable rise of the Conservative Party's
young Libertarians suggests otherwise.

As suggested in my criticism in the Introduction of the social construction of the label 'New Right', the very conceptual structure of
the 'left/right' dichotomy seems ineradicably flawed. Indeed, this is
precisely the argument of the Libertarians themselves. Murray Rothbard in his 1965 essay 'Left and Right: The Prospects For Liberty'
characterises classical liberalism and the whole Enlightenment project as the original 'Left'. He sees Socialism as an internally contradictory ideology that tries to achieve some of the goals of liberalism
(freedom, an end to class rule, rationality) by the means of the statism of the *ancien régime*.[36]

It is arguable that because the Conservative Party has been historically tied to an ill-defined philosophy and has lacked an explicit ideology, its fluidity and 'open-mindedness' has made it inherently adaptable to different epochs and new sets of ideas. As a party that, to some extent, embraces the Popperian spirit of 'open-mindedness', it can be argued that the Conservatives are able to embrace new world-views more easily than other parties more reliant on rigid ideological foundations.

Following the work of Thomas Kuhn,[37] Libertarianism can be argued to represent a paradigm-shift in terms of what it means to be a Conservative activist. The fact that such a change has occurred among the party's youth, and not its senior members, is understandable. For Kuhn suggested that in both the natural and social sciences revolutionary theories are inevitably tied to the emergence of new generations.

Again conforming to Kuhn's theory, Libertarianism does not simply purport to explain the same old facts in a better and more accurate way, but rather it makes what went before totally meaningless in the minds of its supporters. Viewed as the product of post-modern society and the world of Weberian disenchantment, the movements' attraction for its members can be seen to reside ultimately in its secular, rationalistic nature.

However, just as paradigm-shifts are hard to suppress in a scientific community, so they are difficult to stop in a political party. Against Abrams and Little, it is arguable that one of the main functions of Conservative Party youth groups is to challenge older orthodox opinion and provide fresh intellectual blood. Given the ever changing nature of the world and Conservatism it is their job to adapt and articulate new ideas. In a sense, it is their *raison d'être* to break the 'iron law of ideational oligarchy'.

Nevertheless, it is ironic to think that as the one-time defenders of the feudal aristocracy, imperialism, and even the welfare state, it is the Conservative Party's youth wings who have made what Abrams and Little would call a 'breakthrough' in British youth politics. Indeed, it is even more ironic to think that it has been members of the Conservative Party who have adopted, in Libertarianism, a radical world-view based upon the principles of an ultimately secular and politically anarchic belief system. For Libertarianism is an ideology that questions not only the status quo, but ultimately the very existence of the Conservative Party and the whole political process.

Notes and References

1. Abrams, P., and Little, A., 'The Youth Activist in British Politics', *British Journal of Sociology*, Vol. XVI, No. 4, (1965).
2. In a series of informal, open-ended interviews with 50 ex-members of the FCS, 66% said they had one or more parents who regularly voted for a party other than the Conservatives, and 84% said they had no family tradition of party membership whatsoever.
3. Ex-members of the FCS in interviews continually cited these events as being the points at which they became politically conscious.
4. An ex-member of London region FCS who wishes to remain anonymous in a recorded interview with the author, 1991.
5. Gramsci, A., (1978) *Selections from the Prison Notebooks*, Hoare, O., and Nowell Smith, G., (eds), London, Lawrence and Wishart. See also: Habermas, L. (1976) *Legitimation Crisis*, London, Heinemann. Wolfe, A., (1972) *The Limits of Legitimacy: Political Contradictions of Contemporary Capitalism*, New York, Free Press. Keane, J., (ed.) (1984) *Claus Offe's Contradictions of the Welfare State,* London, Hutchinson. On the subject of stagflation and crisis in Britain during the 1970s see: Leys, C., (1983) *Politics in Britain*, London, Heinemann.
6. See: Hall, S., and Jacques, M., (eds) (1989) *New Times, The Changing Face of Politics in the 1990s*, London, Lawrence and Wishart; Lush, S., and Urry, J., (1987) *The End Of Organised Capitalism*, London, Polity Press; Hall, S., 'Brave new World', in *Marxism Today*, October 1988. Murray, P., 'Life after Henry' (Ford), *Marxism Today*, October 1988. Rustin, M., 'The Politics of Post-Fordism: Or the Trouble with New Times', *New Left Review*, No. 175, May/June 1989.
7. Glendening, M.-H., (1990) *Towards A Post-Modern Conservatism?*. This document was presented by Glendening as an introduction to a series of meetings hosted by the National Association of Conservative Graduates (N.A.C.G.) under the heading of the 'Altered States Initiative'.
8. *New Times, Post-Thatcherism: Britain in the Nineties*, (1990) London Conservative Students, p. 22.
9. Ohmae, K., (1992) *The Borderless World*, London, Fontana, p. 4.
10. Extract from a recorded interview in 1987 with the author.
11. Chris Tame, for example, takes regular daily doses of a variety of vitamin tablets and subscribes to a number of American life extension publications. The British cryonics association affiliated with the American corporation Alcor is virtually run by Libertarians. Russell Whitaker, a member of Alcor and a supporter of the Libertarian Alliance, has said in conversation with the author: 'After only limited social interaction with most Alcor members it soon becomes obvious that the majority are Libertarians politically.'
12. Nicholas, D., (1991) *Immortality: Liberty's Final Frontier*, Cultural Notes No. 27., London, Libertarian Alliance, p. 1.
13. Ibid.
14. Ibid., p. 3.
15. Sheskin, A., (1979) *Cryonics: A Sociology of Death and Bereavement*, New York, Irvington Publishers Inc, p. 84.
16. According to Chris Tame of the Libertarian Alliance, in conversation with the author: 'A disproportionately large number of Libertarians have a fascination with, and a passion for, science fiction.'
17. In his essay 'The Science Fiction Novel' quoted in Pierce, J. J., 'Science Fiction and the Romantic Tradition', *Different*, Vol. 3, No. 3, October 1968, p. 24.
18. Tame, C. R., (1986) *Life, Liberty and The Stars: The Ideological Significance of Science Fiction*, Cultural Notes, No. 6, London, Libertarian Alliance, p. 1. Reprinted from: *Science and Public Policy*, The Journal of the Science Policy Foundation, Vol. II, No. 5, October 1984.

19. In his essay 'The Science Fiction Novel' in Pierce, J. J., 'Science Fiction', p. 32.
20. In a review in *Analog*, February 1968; quoted in Pierce, J. J., 'Science Fiction'.
21. Nicholas, D., 'Immortality', p. 4.
22. Gale, D., 'Meet the Extropians', *GQ Magazine* (UK edition), June 1993, pp. 105–60.
23. Ibid., pp. 107–160.
24. Extract from a recorded interview in 1987 with the author.
25. Appleyard, B., in *The Times*, 16 September 1992, p. 14.
26. See, for example: McKenzie, R. T., (1966) *British Political Parties: The Distribution of Power within the Conservative and Labour Parties*, 2nd edn, London, Heinemann. Norton, P., and Aughey, A., (1981) *Conservatives and Conservatism*, London, Temple Smith, Chapter V.
27. See: Kelly, N. R., (1989) *Conservative Party Conferences: The Hidden System*, Manchester, Manchester University Press. See also: Norton, P., and Aughey, A., *Conservatives and Conservatism*, pp. 206–8, 257, 260–61.
28. Michels, R., (1949) *Political Parties*, Glencoe, The Free Press.
29. Argument taken from a recorded interview with Brian Micklethwait and the author in 1991.
30. Although, as Colin Leys has argued 'Clause IV' has always been interpreted by the Labour Party's leadership as a way of achieving a 'more regulated form of capitalism rather than overthrowing it', it nevertheless provides the party with a yardstick against which policy can be formulated and examined. Leys, C., *Politics in Britain*, p. 173. Similarly, Samuel Beer has argued that, unlike those of the Conservatives, Labour Party politics are embodied within a 'syndrome' of political ideas based upon the principles of egalitarianism and participation. Beer, S. H., (1965) *Modern British Politics: A Study of Parties and Pressure Groups*, London, Faber.
31. Extract from a recorded interview in 1991 with the author.
32. Huntington, Samuel, P., (1964) 'Conservatism as an Ideology', in Stankiewicz, W. J., *Political Thought Since World War II*, New York, Free Press, p. 362.
33. Ibid.
34. Abrams, P., and Little, A., 'The Youth Activist', p. 320.
35. Ibid.
36. See Rothbard, 'Left and Right: The Prospects for Liberty', originally in *Left and Right*, Vol. 1, No. 1, Spring 1965 and reprinted in *Egalitarianism as a Revolt Against Nature and Other Essays,* Wahington DC, Libertarian Review Press.
    This is also the argument of Chris Tame in his 'The New Enlightenment' and 'What to Read', in Seldon, A. (ed.), (1985) *The 'New Right' Enlightenment*, Seveoaks, Kent, Economic and Literary Books Ltd. Other criticisms of the 'left/right' dichotomy have been made by Brittan, S., (1968) in *Left or Right: The Bogus Dilemma*, London, Secker and Warburg, and 'Further Thoughts on Left and Right', in Brittan, S., (1973) *Capitalism and the Permissive Society*, London, Macmillan, and by O'Keeffe, D., 'Left and Right: An Outmoded Vocabulary', Libertarian Alliance Conference, 'Social Theory and Freedom', 23 March, 1991.
37. Kuhn, T. S., (1962) *The Structure of Scientific Revolutions*, Chicago, Chicago University Press.

APPENDIX I
Segregation Indices of Class and Religious Background

....

NB: Segregation Index is the sum of the absolute differences divided by 2.

A. CLASS

Class	Students %	Youth Population %	Segregation Index
I	21	19	-2
II	49	35	-14
IIIa	11	30	+19
IIIb	12	8	-4
IV	6	3	-3
V	1	2	+1
	100	97	43/2 = 21.5

Class	Students %	New Wave %	Segregation Index
I	21	22	+1
II	49	33	-16
IIIa	11	27	+16
IIIb	12	9	-3
IV	6	2	-4
V	1	2	+1
	100	95	41/2 = 20.5

Class	Youth Population %	New Wave %	Segregation Index
I	19	22	+3
II	35	33	-2
IIIa	30	27	-3
IIIb	8	9	+1
IV	3	2	-1
V	2	2	+0
	97	95	10/2 = 5.0

B. RELIGION AND SECULARISM

Affiliation	Youth Population %	New Wave %	Segregation Index
Atheism	18.5	20.8	+2.3
Agnosticism	20.3	31.7	+11.4
Religious	61.2	47.5	-13.7
Total	100.0	100.0	27.4/2 = 13.7

Affiliation	Youth Population %	Wets %	Segregation Index
Atheism	18.5	13.3	-5.2
Agnosticism	20.3	13.3	-7.0
Religious	61.2	73.3	+12.1
Total	100.0	99.9	24.3/2 = 12.2

Affiliation	Wets %	New Wave %	Segregation Index
Atheism	13.3	20.8	+7.5
Agnosticism	13.3	31.7	+17.4
Religious	73.3	47.5	-25.8
Total	99.9	100.0	50.7/2 = 25.4

C. RELIGIOUS AFFILIATION

Religious Affiliation	Youth Population %	New Wave %	Segregation Index
C. of Scotland	6.4	8.3	+1.9
Catholic	16.3	10.4	5.9
Jewish	6.4	8.3	+1.9
Methodist	7.0	4.2	-2.8
Muslim	0.0	0.0	0.0
Other	5.8	12.5	+6.7
Total	100.0	100.0	$21.0/2 = 10.5$

Religious Affiliation	Youth Population %	Wets %	Segregation Index
C. of England	58.1	54.5	-3.6
C. of Scotland	6.4	0.0	-6.4
Catholic	16.3	8.2	+1.9
Jewish	6.4	0.0	-6.4
Methodist	7.0	18.2	+11.2
Muslim	0.0	0.0	0.0
Other	5.8	9.1	+3.3
Total	100.0	100.0	$32.8/2 = 16.4$

Religious Affiliation	New Wave %	Wets %	Segregation Index
C. of England	56.3	54.5	+1.8
C. of Scotland	8.3	0.0	+8.3
Catholic	10.4	8.2	-7.8
Jewish	8.3	0.0	+8.3
Methodist	4.2	18.2	-14.0
Muslim	0.0	0.0	0.0
Other	2.5	9.1	+3.4
Total	100.0	100.0	$43.6/2 = 21.8$

APPENDIX II

LEADERSHIP ELECTION LIST

Alex Aiken
Kenneth Baker
Peter Bottomley
Richard Branson
George Bush
Fidel Castro
Alan Clark
Kenneth Clarke
Edwina Curry
Stephen Dorrell
Pro-Europe
Milton Friedman
Michael Forsyth
Apart from Leonard Peikoff? Eric Forth
Sir Marcus Fox
Marc-Henri Glendening
Mikhail Gorbachev
Teresa Gorman
John Gummer
Jim Hacker
Friedrich A. Hayek
Michael Heseltine
William Hague
Michael Howard
Douglas Hurd
It Depends
Tim Janman
Victor Kiam
Tom King
John Knott
Norman Lamont
Peter Lilley
John Major

Francis Maude
Me
David Mellor
Asil Nadir
No One At Moment
Chris Patten
Cecil Parkinson
Madsen Pirie
Michael Portillo
Enoch Powell is too old
Ayn Rand
John Redwood
Nicholas Ridley
Murray Rothbard
Arnold Schwarzenegger
Self
Gillian Shepherd
Adam Smith
Norman Tebbit
Dennis Thatcher
Margaret Thatcher
David Waddington
William Waldegrave
Peter Walker
A Woman
Another Woman One Day

BIBLIOGRAPHIC LIST OF BOOKS AND ARTICLES

....

Abcarian, G., and Stanage, S. M., 'Alienation and the Radical Right', *The Journal of Politics*, Vol. 27, November, (1965).

Abrams, P., and Little, A., 'The Youth Activist in British Politics', *British Journal of Sociology*, Vol. XVI, No. 4, (1965).

Adorno, T. W., Frenkel-Brunswik, E., Levinson, D. J., and Sanford, R. N., (1950) *The Authoritarian Personality*, New York, Harper and Row.

Amery, L. S., (1923) *National and Imperial Economics*, London, The National Unionist Association.

Anderton, P., (1986) *Drug Abuse: Appearance, Reality and Treatment*, Political Notes, No. 2, London, Libertarian Alliance.

Anonymous, (1986) *Armageddon*, 3 Chester Street, Edinburgh, SCCO.

Barry, N. P., (1979) *Hayek's Social and Economic Philosophy*, London, Macmillan.

Becker, G. (1971) *The Economics of Discrimination*, 2nd edn, Chicago, University of Chicago Press.

Beer, S. H., (1965) *Modern British Politics: A Study of Parties and Pressure Groups*, London, Faber.

Benson, B. L., (1990) *The Enterprise of Law: Justice Without the State*, San Francisco, Pacific Research Institute for Public Policy.

Black Flag, (1985–86) Nos. 155, 156, 160.

Boaz, D., (ed.) (1987) *Left, Right and Babyboom*, Washington D. C., CATO Institute.

Bosanquet, N., (1983) *After the New Right*, London, Heinemann.

Branden, B., (1986) *The Passion of Ayn Rand*, London, W. H. Allen and Co.

Branden, N., (1985) *Judgement Day: My Years With Ayn Rand*, New York, Houghton Mifflin.

Branden, N., and Branden, B., (1964) *Who is Ayn Rand?*, New York, Paperback Library.

Briskman, L., (1988) *Two Cheers For Ideology*, Scottish Young Conservatives, Edinburgh.

Brittan, S., (1968) *Left or Right: The Bogus Dilemma*, London, Secker and Warburg.

____, (1973) *Capitalism and the Permissive Society*, London, Macmillan.

Burke, E., (1912) *Reflections on the Revolution in France*, London, Dent, first published 1790.

____, (1962) *An Appeal from the New Whigs to the Old*, New York, Indianapolis, first published in 1791.

Burns, M., 'Who's Right', (1989) *The Scottish Conservative Collegiate Forum 1989 Conference Magazine*.

Butler, E. (1983) *Hayek: His Contribution to the Political and Economic Thought of our Time*, Hounslow, Temple Smith.

Cambell, D., et al., 'Destabilising The Decent People' in *New Statesman*, 15 February 1980.

Chacksfield, A., (1991) *Open The Door! The Case for Abolishing All Immigration Controls*, Political Notes No. 61, London, Libertarian Alliance.

Christie, R., and Jahoda, M., (eds) (1954) *Studies in the Scope and Method of The Authoritarian Personality*, Glencoe, Ill., Free Press.

Clarke, A., (1991) *The Precarious Influence of British Royalty*, Historical Notes No. 14, London, Libertarian Alliance.

_____, (1992) *The Micropolitics of Free Market Money: A Proposal*, Economic Notes No. 39, London, Libertarian Alliance.

Coats, W. L., 'The Economics of Discrimination', *Modern Age*, 1974, 18(1).

Conti, J. G., and Stetson, B., (1993) *Challenging the Civil Rights Establishment: Profiles of a New Black Vanguard*, Praeger Books, Westport, Conn.

Crabbe, B. D., 'Are Authoritarians Sick?' in Ray, J. J., (ed.) (1974) *Conservatism As Heresy*, NSW, Australia and New Zealand Book Co.

Crozier, B., (1993) *Free Agent: The Unseen War 1941–1991*, London, Harper Collins.

Den Uyl, D., and Rasmussen, D. B., (eds) (1986) *The Philosophic Thought of Ayn Rand*, Illinois, Illinois University Press.

Dolan, E. G., (ed.) (1976) *The Foundations of Modern Austrian Economics*, Kansas City, Sheed & Ward.

Dowd, K., (1988) *Private Money*, Hobart Paper No. 112, London, Institute of Economic Affairs.

Dunn, W. C., 'Adam Smith and Edmund Burke: Complimentary Contemporaries', *Southern Economic Journal*, Vol. VII, No. 3, January 1941.

Dwork, D., (1987) *War Is Good For Babies and Other Young Children*, London, Tavistock Publications.

Federation of Conservative Students 'Campaign to Smash the Red Menace' (1984) *The Gordon Liddy Guide to Disrupting NUS Conference.*

Federation of Conservative Students, (1985) *Motions to Conference.*

Federation of Conservatives Students (1986) *FCS Conference Motions: Scarborough.*

Friedman, M., (1962) *Capitalism and Freedom*, Chicago, The University Press.

Friedman, M., and Friedman, R., (1980) *Free to Choose*, Harmondsworth, Penguin Books.

Friedman, M., and Friedman, R., (1985) *The Tyranny of the Status Quo,* Harmondsworth, Penguin Books.

Gale, D., 'Meet the Extropians', *GQ Magazine* (UK edition), June 1993.

Gamble, A., (1979) 'The Free Economy and the strong state: the rise of the social market economy', in Milliband, R., and Saville, J., (eds) *The Socialist Register*, London, Merlin Press.

(1983) 'Thatcherism and Conservative Politics' in Hall, Stuart, and Jacques, Martin, (eds) *The Politics of Thatcherism*, London, Lawrence and Wishart.

Glendening, M., (1990) *Towards A Post-Modern Conservatism?*, National Association of Conservative Graduates.

Gordon, P., and Klug, F., (1986) *New Right, New Racism*, London, Searchlight Publications.

Graham, D., and Clarke, P. (1986) *The New Enlightenment*, London, Macmillan in association with Channel 4.

Gramsci, A., (1978) *Selections from the Prison Notebooks*, Hoare, O., and Nowell Smith, G., (eds), London, Lawrence and Wishart.

Grassl, W., and Smith, B., (eds) (1986) *Austrian Economics*, London, Croom Helm.

Greater London Young Conservatives (1988) *GLYC Report of the Representatives to the National Advisory Committee.*

Green, D., (1985) *Working Class Patients and the Medical Establishment*, Hounslow, Temple Smith.

Habermas, L., (1976) *Legitimation Crisis*, London, Heinemann.

Hall, S., 'Brave new World', in *Marxism Today*, October 1988.

Hall, S., and Jacques, M., (eds) (1989) *New Times, The Changing Face of Politics in the 1990s*, London, Lawrence and Wishart.

Hayek, F. A., (1944) *The Road to Serfdom*, London, Routledge and Kegan Paul.

——, (1976) *Law, Legislation and Liberty*, London, Routledge and Kegan Paul.

——, (1978) *Denationalisation of Money: The Argument Refined*, Hobart Paper No. 70, London, Institute of Economic Affairs.

——, (1978) *New Studies in Philosophy, Politics and Economics*, London, Routledge & Kegan Paul.

——, (1980) *Individualism and Economic Order*, Chicago, University of Chicago Press, Midway reprint.

——, (1984) *Money, Capital and Fluctuations*, R, McCloughry (ed.), London, Routledge.

Heinlein, R., (1969) *The Moon is a Harsh Mistress*, London, Hodder and Stoughton Ltd, New English Library.

Hirsch, F., (1977) *The Social Limits to Growth*, Cambridge MA, Harvard University Press.

Hofstadter, R., (1955) 'The Pseudo-Conservative Revolt', in Bell. D., *The New American Right*, New York, Criterion Books.

Horwitz, T., (1967) *The Political Economy of South Africa*, London, Weidenfeld and Nicolson.

Hull University and Humberside College Federation of Conservative Students, (1986) *The Right Handbook.*

Huntington, S. P., (1964) 'Conservatism as an Ideology', in Stankiewicz, W. J., *Political Thought Since World War II*, Free Press, New York.

Hutt, W. H., (1964) *The Economics of the Colour Bar*, London, Andre Deutsch and Institute of Economic Affairs.

Jamieson, L., and Corr, H., (eds) (1990) *State, Private Life and Political Change*, London, Macmillan.

Jones, G., (1980) *Social Darwinism and English Thought*, Brighton, Harvester Press.

(1989) *Social Hygiene in Twentieth Century Britain*, London, Croom Helm.

Keane, J., (ed.) (1984) *Claus Offe's Contradictions of the Welfare State*, London, Hutchinson.

Kelly, R., (1989) *Conservative Party Conferences: The Hidden System*, Manchester, Manchester University Press.

Kirkpatrick, J., (1982) *Dictatorships and Double Standards*, New York, Simon and Schuster.

Kirzner, I., (1986) *Subjectivism, Intelligibility and Economic Understanding*, London, Macmillan.

Kuhn, T. S., (1962) *The Structure of Scientific Revolutions*, Chicago, Chicago University Press.

Lachmann, L. M., (1977) *Capital, Expectations and Market Process*, Kansas City, Sheed, Andrews & McMeel.

Layton-Henry, Z., (1980) *Conservative Party Politics*, Basingstoke, MacMillan.

Levitas, R., (1986) 'Tory Students and the New Right', *Youth and Policy*, No. 16.

Levitas, R., (ed.) (1986) *The Ideology of the New Right*, Oxford, Polity Press.

Lewis, R., et al, (1986) *Apartheid – Capitalism or Socialism?*, London, Institute of Economic Affairs.

Leys, C., (1983) *Politics in Britain*, London, Heinemann.

London Conservative Students, (1988) *Defenders of Liberty Handbook*, London, Greater London Area Conservative Collegiate Forum.

London Conservative Students, (1990) *New Times, Post-Thatcherism: Britain in the Nineties*.

Lush, S., and Urry, J., (1987) *The End Of Organised Capitalism*, London, Polity Press.

Macmillan, H., (1938) *The Middle Way*, London, Macmillan & Co.

Maddox, W. S., and Lilie, S. A., (1989) *Beyond Liberal and Conservative: Reassessing the Political Spectrum*, Washington DC, CATO Institute.

Marks, P., (1994) *The Principled Libertarianism of Edmund Burke (1929–1979)*, Libertarian Heritage No. 13, London, Libertarian Alliance.

Martin, J. J., (1970) *Men Against the State: The Expositors of Individualist Anarchism in America 1827–1908*, Colorado Springs, Ralph Myles Publisher.

Marx, K., and Engels, F., (1848) *Manifest der Kommunistischen Partei*. Authorised English translation by Samuel Moore, with introduction and notes by Engels (1888).

McKenzie, R. T., (1966) *British Political Parties: The Distribution of Power within the Conservative and Labour Parties*, 2nd edn, London, Heinemann.

Mevrill, R. E., (1991) *The Ideas of Ayn Rand*, La Salle, Illinois, Open Court.

Michels, R., (1949) *Political Parties*, Glencoe, The Free Press.

Micklethwait, B., (1983) *In Praise of Mercenaries*, Political Notes No. 11, London, Libertarian Alliance.

_____, (1987) *Taking Free Market Defence Seriously*, Foreign Policy Perspectives No.7, London, Libertarian Alliance.

_____, (1991) *How and How Not to Demonopolise Medicine*, Political Notes No. 56., London, Libertarian Alliance.

_____, (1993) *How and How Not to Achieve Good Taste in Advertising: Free Market Regulation is Better than Government Regulation*, Political Notes No. 74, London, Libertarian Alliance.

Mises, L., von (1966) *Human Action*, 3rd revised edn, Chicago, Contemporary Books.

_____, (1978) *Ultimate Foundations of Economic Science*, Kansas City, Sheed, Andrews & McMeel.

_____, (1981) *Socialism*, Indianapolis, Liberty Fund.

Moulin, M., (1985/6) *Blueprint*, Greater London Young Conservatives.

Murray, P., 'Life after Henry' (Ford), *Marxism Today*, October 1988.

National Union of Conservative and Unionist Associations, (1987) *104th Conservative Conference Handbook*, London.

National Union of Conservative and Unionist Associations, (1981) *Report of the Committee of Inquiry Concerning the Federation of Conservative Students*.

Nicholas, D., (1991) *Immortality: Liberty's Final Frontier*, Cultural Notes No. 27, London, Libertarian Alliance.

Nisbet, R. A., 'De Bonald and the Concept of the Socil Group', *Journal of the History of Ideas*, Vol. V, No. 3, June 1944.

Nisbet, R. A., 'Conservatism and Sociology', *American Journal of Sociology*, Vol. LVIII, No. 2, September 1952.

Northam, R., (1939) *Conservatism the Only Way*, The Right Book Club, London.

Norton, P., and Aughey, A., (1981) *Conservatives and Conservatism*, London, Temple
    Smith.
Nozick, R., (1974) *Anarchy, State and Utopia*, Oxford, Basil Blackwell.
O'Brien, C. C., (1992) *The Great Melody: A Thematic Biography and Commented
    Anthology of Edmund Burke*, Oxford, Sinclair Stevenson.
O'Hara, (1994) *Lie Too Far: Searchlight, Hepple and the Left*, London, Mina Enterprise,
    London.
Ohmae, K., (1992) *The Borderless World*, London, Fontana.
Oppenheimer, F., (1926) *The State*, New York, Vanguard Press.
Pearce, E., 'Royalty For Grown-ups, in Phibbs, H., (ed.) *New Agenda*, Federation of
    Conservative Students (London Region), Vol. 1, No. 2, Winter 1985–1986.
Pejovich, S., and Klingamen, D., (eds) (1975) *Individual Freedom: Selected Works of W.
    H. Hutt*, Westport, Connecticut, Greenwood Press.
Pierce, J. J., 'Science Fiction and the Romantic Tradition', *Different*, Vol. 3, No. 3,
    October 1968.
Pirie, M., 'The Cross of St Andrews' in *Freedom First: The Journal of the Society for
    Individual Freedom*, No. 76, Summer 1989.
____, (1992) *Blueprint for a Revolution*, London, Adam Smith Institute (Research) Ltd.
Rabushka, A., (1974) *A Theory of Racial Harmony*, Carolina, University of South
    Carolina Press.
Ramsay, R., (1992) 'Our Searchlight Problem', *Lobster*, No. 24, December 1992.
Rand, A., (1943) *The Fountainhead*, New York, The Bobbs-Merrill Company.
____, (1961) *For the New Intellectual*, New York, Signet Books.
____, (1964) *The Virtue of Selfishness*, New York, New American Library.
____, (1967) 'What is Capitalism?' in *Capitalism the Unknown Ideal*, New York, New
    American Library.
Rothbard, M. N., 'Left and Right: The Prospects for Liberty', *Left and Right*, Vol. 1,
    No. 1, Spring 1965.
'The Anatomy of The State' in *Rampart Journal of Individualist Thought*, Vol. 1, No. 2,
    Summer, 1965.
(1973) *For a New Liberty*, New York, The Macmillan Publishing Co.
Rothbard, M. N., (ed.) (1987) *The Review of Austrian Economics*, Vol.1, Lexington,
    Mass, D. C. Heath.
Rush, G, B., 'Toward A Definition of the Extreme Right', in *Pacific Sociological
    Review*, Fall, 1963.
Rustin, M., 'The Politics of Post-Fordism: Or the Trouble with New Times', *New Left
    Review*, No. 175, May/June 1989.
Schuman, H., and Presser, S., (1981) *Questions and Answers in Attitude Surveys*, New
    York, Academic Press.
Scottish Conservative Students, (1990) *Media Training Guide*.
Scottish Conservative Students, (1990) *Capitalist Worker*, Spring Term.
Scottish Federation of Conservative Students, (1986) *A Conservative Manifesto for
    Scotland*, 3 Chester Street, Edinburgh, SCCO.
Searle, G. R., (1971) *The Quest for National Efficiency*, Oxford, Oxford University
    Press.
____, (1976) *Eugenics and Politics in Britain 1900–1914*, Leyden, Noordoff
    International Publishing.
Seldon, A.,(1991) 'Freedom, Responsibility and Justice: The Criminology of the
    New Right', in Stenson, K., and Cowell, D., (eds) *The Politics of Crime Control*,
    London, Sage Publications.

Seldon, A., (ed.) (1985) *The New Right Enlightenment,* Sevenoaks, Kent, Economic and Literary Books.

Semmel, B., (1960) *Imperialism and Social Reform: English Social Imperial Thought 1895–1914,* Harvard, Harvard University Press.

Shand, A. H., (1990) *Free Market Morality: The Political Economy of the Austrian School,* London, Routledge.

Sheskin, A., (1979) *Cryonics: A Sociology of Death and Bereavement,* New York, Irvington Publishers Inc.

Skocpol, T., (1992) *Protecting Soldiers and Mothers: The Political Origins of Social Policy in the United States,* Belknap Press/Harvard University Press.

Smedley, I., (1990) 'One Hell of a Party,' in Gray, P., (ed.) *Campaigner: The Magazine of the National Young Conservatives,* London, Youth Department, Conservative Central Office.

Soloway, R. A., (1990) *Demography and Degeneration: Eugenics and the Declining Birthrate in Twentieth Century Britain,* Chapel Hill, University of North Carolina Press.

Sowell, T., (1972) *Black Education: Myths and Tragedy,* New York, David McKay.

———, (1979) *Race and Economics,* London, Longman.

———, (1981) *Markets and Minorities,* Oxford, Basil Blackwell.

———, (1984) *Civil Rights: Rhetoric or Reality,* New York, William Morrow.

———, (1987) *Compassion Versus Guilt,* New York, William Morrow.

———, (1994) *Is Reality Optional? and Other Essays,* Stanford, Hoover Institution.

Sowell, T., (ed.) (1980) *American Ethnic Groups,* Washington DC, The Urban Institute.

Spadaro, L. M., (ed.) (1978) *New Directions in Austrian Economics,* Kansas City, Sheed, Andrews & McMeel.

Staines, P., (1991) *Acid House Parties Against The Lifestyle Police and the Safety Nazis,* Political Notes No. 55, London, Libertarian Alliance.

Stankiewicz, W. J., (ed.) (1964) *Political Thought Since World War Two,* New York, Free Press.

Tame, C. R., (1980) *Bibliography of Freedom,* London, Centre for Policy Studies.

———, (1986) *Life, Liberty and The Stars: The Ideological Significance of Science Fiction,* Cultural Notes, No. 6, London, Libertarian Alliance.

Therbon, G., 'West On The Dole', in *Marxism Today,* June 1985.

Thomas, R., (1991) *The Nature of Nazi Ideology,* Historical Notes, No. 15, London, Libertarian Alliance.

———, (1994) 'Edmund Burke, Liberty and Drugs', *Free Life: A Journal of Classical Liberal and Libertarian Thought,* No. 21, London, Libertarian Alliance.

Tucker, B., (1893) *Instead of a Book,* New York.

Warren, J., (1846) *Equitable Commerce,* New Harmony.

———, (1863) *True Civilization,* Boston.

Wassenarr, A. D., (1977) *Assault on Private Enterprise,* Cape Town, Tafelberg Publishers.

Williams, W., 'Government Sanctioned Restraints That Reduce Economic Opportunities for Minorities', *Policy Review,* 1977, No. 2.

'Racism and Organised Labour', *Lincoln Review,* 1979.

———, (1982) *The State Against Blacks,* New York, McGraw Hill.

———, (1989) *South Africa's War Against Capitalism,* Westport, Connecticut, Praeger.

Wolfe, A., (1972) *The Limits of Legitimacy: Political Contradictions of Contemporary Capitalism,* New York, Free Press.

Woodcock, G., (1977) *The Anarchist Reader,* Hassocks, Sussex, The Harvester Press.

Wortham, A., 'Equal Opportunity Versus Individual Opportunity', *The Freeman*, July 1975.

Wortham, A., 'Individuality and Intellectual Independence', *The Freeman*, August 1975.

_____, 'Response to "A Black Writer's View of Roots"', *Reason*, 1977, 9(1).

_____, 'A Black Writer's View of 'Roots'', *Libertarian Forum*, March 1977, X(3).

_____, 'An Open Letter to Nathan Glazer', *Reason*, 1977, 9(5).

_____, 'A Decision Against Meritorious Achievement', *The Freeman*, August 1978, 28(10).

_____, (1981) *The Other Side of Racism: A Philosophical Study of Black Race Consciousness*, Ohio, Ohio State University Press.

INDEX